The Wet Collection

The
Wet
Collection

Joni Tevis

MILKWEED EDITIONS

Untitled (Pharmacy), 1943. Joseph Cornell. Construction, 15-1/4 × 12 × 3-1/8. Collection Mrs. Marcel Duchamp, Paris.

Cover art © The Joseph and Robert Cornell Memorial Foundation/Licensed by VAGA, New York, NY

Published 2012 by Milkweed Editions
Printed in the United States
Cover design by Christian Fuenfhausen
Author photo by David Bernardy
Interior design by Wendy Holdman
The text of this book is set in Adobe Caslon Pro.
12 13 14 15 16   5 4 3 2 1
First Paperback Edition
ISBN: 978-1-57131-316-4

Special funding for this book was provided by the Jerome Foundation.

Milkweed Editions, a nonprofit publisher, gratefully acknowledges sustaining support from Emilie and Henry Buchwald; the Bush Foundation; the Patrick and Aimee Butler Family Foundation; CarVal Investors; the Timothy and Tara Clark Family Charitable Fund; the Dougherty Family Foundation; the Ecolab Foundation; the General Mills Foundation; the Claire Giannini Fund; John and Joanne Gordon; William and Jeanne Grandy; the Jerome Foundation; Dorothy Kaplan Light and Ernest Light; Constance B. Kunin; Marshall BankFirst Corp.; Sanders and Tasha Marvin; the May Department Stores Company Foundation; the McKnight Foundation; a grant from the Minnesota State Arts Board, through an appropriation by the Minnesota State Legislature, a grant from the National Endowment for the Arts, and private funders; an award from the National Endowment for the Arts, which believes that a great nation deserves great art; the Navarre Corporation; Debbie Reynolds; the St. Paul Travelers Foundation; Ellen and Sheldon Sturgis; the Target Foundation; the Gertrude Sexton Thompson Charitable Trust (George R. A. Johnson, Trustee); the James R. Thorpe Foundation; the Toro Foundation; Moira and John Turner; United Parcel Service; Joanne and Phil Von Blon; Kathleen and Bill Wanner; Serene and Christopher Warren; the W. M. Foundation; and the Xcel Energy Foundation.

The Library of Congress has catalogued the hardcover edition as follows:

Tevis, Joni.
    The wet collection / Joni Tevis. — 1st ed.
        p.   cm.
    Includes bibliographical references.
    ISBN 978-1-57131-303-4 (acid-free paper)
    I. Title.
PS3620.E95W48 2007
811'.6—dc22
                                        2007007232

This book is printed on acid-free,
recycled (100% postconsumer waste)
paper.

For my parents,

Earl Lee Tevis

and

Margie Ann (Moore) Tevis

Contents

III.

Epilogue

The Wet Collection

Prologue

The Wet Collection

The bellies of the birds—phoebe, grackle, redwing blackbird—have been stitched in neat zigzags from crop to throat. Someone's patient hand pinched the lips of the emptied breast. Someone pushed insecticide-laced batting into the cavity. Someone tied the knot.

Here, in the basement of the natural history museum, they understand the virtues of careful storage. The vaults hold hundreds of birds, stuffed and shelved for study. People bring what they find: sparrows, mourning doves, the common birds of the city. Then someone eviscerates the dead thing, sprinkles cornmeal to soak the blood, glues cabochons of glass for the eyes.

This is work that few see. We are here only because the quiet curator took an hour from her afternoon's work to show us around. Handwritten notes line a drawer of eggs from a donated private collection. One note, written in a deliberate script in faded brown ink, reads: "Collected under a clump of grass approximately 3 feet from a pasture road. A. S. Wilson, 1919." This in a curving, fountain-pen script nobody has any more. What now of the pasture road? Is it there still; is it a superhighway? The egg, so fragile, and its clump of grass remain after the man and the world he noted so carefully have vanished.

The wet collection is a well-stocked pantry, its shelves full of ranked bottles and jars. There are capped plastic drums of paper-wrapped voles, evidence of a research paper (now abandoned) on the boom and crash of vole populations. From vole tails, the trained scientist can determine body-fat percentage and other useful statistics. As the vole goes, so go the vole's predators: owl, badger, fox. One jar is jammed full of skinless, headless, eyeless carcasses. Someone cut out corneas, but we don't know why. A vole's eyes are small and black, stubby as pencil points.

Another shelf holds jarfuls of dried tongues: flamingo, great blue heron, crowned and sandhill crane, American bittern, and roseate spoonbill in one; in another, woodcock and woodpecker, desiccated, labels tied to each with pieces of thread (collected 1952, 1961). They should be packed in salt, these scraps of dried flesh, like capers or artichoke hearts. A moose's wide tongue floats in alcohol.

An old pickle jar holds the face and long, bent ears of a jackrabbit. Where its eyes should be there are only bits of skin, blank and white. The stuff of nightmares. When we walk past, dark-tipped guard hairs wave in the jar's yellowish fluid. The curator locks the door behind us.

There is something repulsive in this, these parts taken without a whole. We have tongues but no cranes, tails without voles and caches of grain, a tattered seagull but no sand or waves or thermal air current, and without these things, the jars are full of creatures eminently dead, mere fragments enshrined. The snapping turtle with two heads is misplaced no matter where it sits.

And yet. The curator lifts the dead grebe carefully from its place, reads the label she wrote long ago. Fingers the down. She slides the drawer shut and opens another, this one holding cedar waxwings. *Some of them still have red tips on the wings,* she says, and picks up one after the other until she finds one that does. *Like flecks of house paint.* Spatters so small you'd never see them in the field. Pilgrims with their relics are not more respectful. Long years of handling fragile things have made her touch light; each specimen is secure in her hands. She collects data one piece at a time, her eyes gleaming with facts. The kiwi, whose egg is a third as large as its body, breathes through the end of its beak. The star-nosed mole's twenty-seven tentacles, tipped with electrical sensors, help it find earthworms, its favorite food. See and touch the ostrich egg, pocked and dimpled like grapefruit skin; see the praying mantis—also called the devil's rearhorse, or soothsayer, or mule killer—pinned to balsa wood. Careful study is a holy work.

Before we leave, the curator tells us about her first job at the museum, transferring to tiny labels field notes someone else had taken. She recorded genus and species, collection date, location, in miniscule handwriting with a fine-pointed pen. Someone else matched specimen with label. *The hours I spent,* she says, *keeping records on animals I would never see.* It has been a long time since I've seen such faith. Wishing us well, she turns to her work, and we show ourselves out and up to street level, leaving the collections behind.

Today I'm thinking of the quiet curator, secular mystic, care her creed and discipline. In her basement room she records the mysteries we'd miss otherwise. Sometimes I'm stopped cold by dragonflies—devil's darning needles, snake doctors—rising in glittering clouds to scatter, sun flashing from taut wings, over streets littered with God's dropped handkerchiefs, scribbled notes.

I.

A Field Guide to Iridescence and Memory

What Are You Looking For?

Something of interest—overlooked, easily missed. Memory reveals itself in flashes: a red window of blurred desert, skin stained and pricked by wild blackberries. Eyes open for the image that summons the memory.

Getting Started and Setting Out

My favorite chapter in any field guide. What to pack in the canvas bag? Newsprint for wrapping specimens; sandwich and canteen; a hat to cheat the sun; notebook and reliable ink. Keeping notes in the field is the hallmark of the dedicated student. Otherwise, once home, you'll unpack nothing but a bag of rocks. Your notes will provide context, nail down ephemera (creek bed, mile 1.2, partially immersed, waterline). Your notes will be the record that survives you.

Bring silence, and an ear tuned to slight differences. Bring palms embedded with grit; bring water. Comb the world for clues. The banded agate damp with lake water, crusted with sand: get close, peering, picking through. Find the pottery shard hid in dirt; find the dirt. Exile is a condition of the redeemed life. Remember: you find what you look for; when presented with a fragment, fit a builded life to it. Line the pieces up and study them, catalogue and compare. Remember to keep careful notes. In India ink, which resists fade and run.

Specimen: Damselfly

The shape of a flattened oval, another; a pair, cut clean, as by newly sharpened shears. Black like deep-pile velvet, rich, topographic: silvery along the wrinkles' ridges, cave-black in the valleys, these wings fused to a peacock-blue stylus. The dying damselfly, shuddering in my palm, her body shining like a radio tube, like a bugle bead, like a Christmas ornament: blown glass lined with aluminum, cheap, yet carefully packed in its nest of crushed paper, waiting for next year.

Specimen: Silk

One night, walking through the woods, I came across a spiderweb big as a hula hoop, anchored to two shortleaf pines. See the magnificent thing, fragile diamond sheet, the maker inverted and swaying, knitting up the gaps. Without pausing, she dropped from one spoke to another, pulling a strand taut, anchoring. The lines, close as a record's grooves, shone violet and lime in the flashlight. She tatted a zigzag of thicker stuff down the middle: a decorative touch, because it delighted her.

Specimen: Black Opals

The camp-host couple showed me their collection that summer in Oregon. They found the stones in Nevada while sifting through a load of earth they'd bought from a mine. They kept the opals in a canning jar of mineral oil, so the pinfire wouldn't fade. When he fished one out with his hard logger's hand, I took it. Fevered walnut, sparking in my palm.

Specimen: Blue Morpho

In the Wonder Room at the Menil Collection, just down the street from my apartment in Houston, was a Riker mount of a blue morpho—rare butterfly of the rain forest pressed under glass, resplendent but radically dead. The color of the butterfly's wings shifted, from sapphire to tourmaline to amethyst.

Then in Costa Rica, on our honeymoon. He flashed between palm trees, lighted on leaves, drank juice from burst fruit. We watched him flicker through the woods with others of his kind. Here's how much larger, more generous, the world can be.

THE IRIDESCENCE OF MEMORY

Take this a step further, when an image pierces the memory and bounces off an answering memory from the past, or a vision of the future. The optical phenomenon of iridescence—rainbows arcing from peacocks or blue morphos—begins with repeated reflections from translucent, ridged surfaces; when the viewer moves, the colors seem to change. The iridescence of memory happens when one image (physical) illuminates another (imagined): not quite a reflection, but a refraction. These visions, these flashes of color come again and again. How then must I live?

MEMORY: FLORENCE, ITALY

A gray Sunday in late winter: damp sheen on the cobblestones, the sharp smell of roasting chestnuts. The piazza wasn't crowded; mass had ended hours before. I had just eaten a bowl of *ribollita,* something I often ordered, because it didn't cost much: torn greens and beef-bone broth, poured over day-old bread. As I walked home, I saw an old man in a gray suit, leading a little boy by the hand. The boy watched the pigeons that jerked and clucked across the square, and when he said something to his grandfather, the old man looked down at him and smiled; maybe he even laughed in appreciation, I don't remember. And suddenly I knew that in watching them I was seeing myself with my grandfather, gone then fifteen years—watching how we had been together, in a quiet corner of the world, unnoticed.

Cared for by women who knew how to stretch a lean budget, how to make things last.

Memory: Prague

After a month in Dresden, Prague looked like a stage set to me, partly an effect of the crenellated architecture, partly a trick of the light—clean, blue-yellow, I'd recognize it anywhere. I couldn't get the history out of my head: April 1945, the Allies firebomb Dresden to the ground, sparing Prague because Winston Churchill had visited once and liked it.

I wandered through the historic district. Crystal beads sparkled in shop windows; I bought a ring carved from a piece of dark wood. As the afternoon waned, the vendors started rolling up their linens and necklaces. That's when I saw her: the woman eating an ice-cream cone. Maybe seventy, she walked alone across the square, taking it all in with the delight of someone on holiday, the ease of someone who'd lived there forever. It's not that she was dancing across the stones, but something about the way she walked said, *Joy to the roots of my hair.*

What I Want

To know what it means to live a biblical life, uncloistered every day. This is my book of new ritual, of learning to live a prophetic life in conjunction with another. Togetherness's attraction and threat—the shared room, common air. My practice is observation. How do relationships illuminate?

Specimen: Pearl

In the middle of March, a heavy, sticking snow fell, clinging to Norway firs and rooftop gutters, capping fire hydrants, rising like bread all over the city. So much for our trip to Florida. We slogged down the street to the café, comforted ourselves with wine. I was eating a mussel when I felt a chip of something in my mouth—grit?—but when I fished with my finger, I found a very small pearl. Outside, a man in a red truck skidded into a snowbank.

The storm started to let up. The sun lowered in a nacreous sky, and I wondered what it meant—that a pearl drops from my tongue like a coal afire, that I roll it on my glottal speech. Not carelessly to be swallowed. Not to be crushed between teeth.

Traveling Alone

After the sad awkwardness of farewell, the day's mine to do with as I like. Doors slide open at my approach. Everything I need I've got, packed in the bag that swings at my side.

I step boldly to the counter, where the ticket agent recites his litany of questions: *have these bags left your possession*; no they have not left my possession; *have you been given anything to transport by persons unknown to you*; I have not been given anything by persons unknown to me. *Are you traveling alone today; what is your ultimate destination?* Scrawling a gate number in grease pencil with a casual movement like an absolution, he sends me on my way.

Today I'm a traveler, a person suspended. Today I'll do only what's asked, writing my address on a tag, showing proof of identity, waiting. *Keep Walking. Do Not Stop or Turn Back* reads the sign. Guiding a bin into the scanner's dark mouth. Removing coat and shoes, passing irradiated through an open door, barefoot as a pilgrim. Allowing bespectacled guards to scrutinize my face, body, belongings, furrow-browed guards rationing words of greeting, dismissing me with a nod.

Other travelers crowd the concourse, some running down the carpeted aisle, some strolling, killing time. Even so, I am alone. I see nobody familiar and would be surprised if I did. Icons line the halls; in a mural, Ronald McDonald pilots an open-cockpit plane as the Hamburgler drops bags of fries on a sleeping city. Snoopy; Starbucks. A city name emblazoned on a T-shirt.

Canny moneymakers, knowing the addictive qualities of distraction, supply the terminals with televisions and cocktail lounges. A woman, paging through a celebrity newsmagazine she will not buy, absently tugs at her necklace. A man stretches across a row of vinyl seats, briefcase pillowing his head, eyes shut. Others talk on phones or fill out crosswords. But I see a few staring into middle distance, eyes on the floor. What do they think of? Can we know each other at all?

Takeoff pushes me back in my seat, amazing me as it always does, this everyday miracle. High above middle America, I see thin roads pressed at even intervals into mountain valleys, brown winter land crumpled and silent. Flashes of green iridescence: highway signs. Pale clusters of cul-de-sacs, roads whorled as fingerprints, cleared red land ready for a new subdivision. "Knoxville," says the captain, and what I see shapes itself into known things, the long plank of Tennessee. Afternoon rushes away from me as I doze in my thinly padded seat, waking when the plane tilts. Now pale snow coats the far ground, and blue-black shadows scallop the hills; a red strand of taillights lines a highway. The moon burns cold behind my ear.

Going home is traveling in time to a life I once had; it should be impossible, wrought by spell casting if at all, to visit these places I see in dreams. A lacebark elm grew outside the east window of that first apartment. Bright sun through its leaves woke me every morning, and its branches rattled the glass during storms. That time is gone. But then I board a plane, and in an afternoon travel back two years or twenty. I press fingertips to the elm, whose branchlets are already, late February, forcing out yellow green leaves. No wonder airports are places of threat and confusion; of freedom, tears, small dramas, and petty cash. Here all times of a life can meld. (When the plane touches down, the attendant reminds the travelers to reset their watches to the proper hour.) Here I recognize no one; my own face, in the restroom mirror, surprises me.

I walk the covered gangway with my fellow travelers. Together we've been shaken by turbulence high above the ground; together we pass through the arrival gate and breathe the stale air of the waiting area with its sealed plate glass windows.

Together we relearn how to walk the curving earth, gliding past those who lean against walls waiting for their flights, or stand in line to buy the local paper with its unfamiliar masthead, or disappear into the hazy enclave of the smokers' lounge. But our temporary solidarity recedes with every step, its last traces floating away as I ascend the escalator, searching the crowd for faces that look a little different every time.

As I walk away from the airport, I keep thinking of the other travelers, nameless to me; we have all stepped through the portal, repeated our throwaway vows. Every trip is in practice for the next. This is how to keep yourself malleable, moving from city to city. Sometimes I think I know these strangers better than those I return to, the ones who never left. Then the day of traveling ends. And I become as they are, until I take up my discipline again.

Jeremiad of a Bad Drought Year

In a wet season, the tulip tree prospers, roots wriggling through humus and pinching slick clay, branches forcing out wrinkled leaves that unfurl, stretch taut, shake down shade on trailing squaw-weed and dark pipsissewa. And the sunlight through leaves is green and gutters when the wind blows. Some, pressing stethoscopes to trunk, say it's possible to hear sap rise; veins groan as they strain, laboring.

In a wet season, the tulip tree swallows sun, is the Appalachian forests' prize. Straight and thick-boled, it would make a good canoe; Cherokee twisted its fibrous bark into fishnets, plaited it into strong rope. Early in the season it drops painted buds to the ground, tender petals dipped in orange, and by this token makes its lineage known: magnolia. The blooms of the famous Southern magnolia, white and peach-smelling, are so delicate they cannot be touched; even careful fingers burn the petals brown.

But in August of a bad drought year, I watched the tulip tree choke on sap curdled from want of rain. Too soon it dropped leaves, bone-colored, to litter the trail like tossed paper; its naked branches rattled. In August of a bad drought year I hiked to the mountaintop, and under my feet frazzled grass crunched, and no beetle buzzed, no snake rustled. My shoes left no print on the hardpack clay. In a wet season, I had seen clouds darken to charcoal there, seen rivers of rain flush the bald clean of ground quartz and pine straw. But this year the trail smelled of baking earth. My feet pounded leaves to dust, and I could not count the dying trees.

2.

He wakes in a dream, tongue thick with dust, robe sweat-damp. He knows where he is: a battleground outside the city, the valley of dry bones. Squinting against the sun, he stares across the plain at the skeleton-stacked canyon, waiting. Then the voice of the Lord rockets across the noontime desert, howling around hoodoos, asking: *O man, will these bones rise again?* What can he say? Ezekiel answers, wisely, *Lord, thou knowest.*

Then it happens: wind blasts down the valley and knocks the bones to the ground. They clatter as they fall, raising dust, and as the wind gusts the bones rise and pair, sorting themselves from their stacks. Bone to bone they twirl and knit, dance like leaves, figure the old fit. Pale at first, sun bleached, the bones redden and sprout sinew, thick cords of muscle, unwrinkled skin.

In the valley of dry bones rises a blank-eyed army. They are the standing dead; their placid faces do not crease in shock, their limp arms do not clutch their chests. Then another, softer wind steals through the valley, and the army of men does live. What they do next we are not told.

3.

On a short summer night in the bad drought year, I walked through dark woods that shivered with lust for the burning. Stars glinted in an obsidian sky, the air too dry to tat a cloud. I kept to the trail, the day's heat still rising from it, and in the darkness saw a lighter stretch ahead. As I walked toward it, the sound of rasping and grinding, quiet at first, grew loud. When I stepped from dark woods into gray light, I was in a clear-cut, pines stacked in ragged piles, snarled roots upended. All around me was the sound of chewing, millions of mouths crunching wood: pine beetles. No bigger than a pencil point but capable of killing thousands of acres, pine beetles love dry years because drought-weakened trees can't fight. To slow the beetles' spread, foresters cut infested trees; when the tree dies, the beetles starve. It stopped me short: the hole in the forest, piles of uprooted trees, and, worst, the infested pines that still stood, their needles tinder dry—an army of the dead. I haven't walked through that clear-cut in years, haven't seen the skinny pioneer species (by the creek, alder; in the sun, Virginia pine) that must be, already, turning the scar into something like forest, but I can't shake the vision I had—gnawing mouths and drifts of sawdust on a blighted midsummer night.

4.

Once, in a wet season, a summer storm caught me on the mountain ridge. Storms can gather fast in the lower Smokies, stalling above the creased gorges; I didn't notice until the air thickened and thunder knocked. The sky drained of color as it will in the long summer dusk—it was a glass of milk, the storm a root clutch steeping there. Then the sky piled like a bolt of denim at the textile mill down the road (the one that shut down after forty hard years: now bearded grasses crack the parking lot, lay raw clay bare), sky unburdened itself like the mill on its last day, when workers packed looms on flatbeds and wrapped them in yellow tarps, and drivers tightened the straps to secure the machines for the long haul down to Mexico. The newly out of work watched the trucks pull out of the lot, making for the freeway, and long after the trucks disappeared the diesel they burned hung heavy in the air. That day on the ridge the sky above the mountains went dark as the abandoned mill's blind exhaust vent, and the screaming of crows was like skittering claws on metal. And then the rains came.

The storm clamped down and set to pounding. Wind ripped through the gorge, bending and shaking the trees, and thunder hummed low like big trucks rolling. Lightning flashed its keen steel scissors. A town girl caught without shelter, I ran down the trail looking for a place to ride it out, found a crevice beneath an overhang and crawled in. Ant lions' conical traps dotted the powdery ground, and dark lampshade spiders crouched against the granite ceiling. Hunched in last year's leaves, I watched the storm erase the trees across the gorge, turn the nearby hemlocks into dark thrashing shapes, sheet the trail next to me with water. Cold rain blew in, and I hugged myself, scared, when thunder split with a sound not like a slammed door or a dropped dictionary, not like a kerosene bomb or a bulldozed wall, not like bent metal screaming: like something inside my head, a nightmare cry pushing out. Lightning flashed close, closer, and when it struck a near hemlock I heard sap sizzle and smelled ozone, then the thunder cracked loud with a sound like earth breaking, and I screamed.

When the storm passed, strips of blue showing through the torn sky, I crawled from my hiding place to hike the slippery trail (broken branches, split trees) down the gorge, where the creek ran thick and fast, yellow with mud, over swells of boulders. Carefully I pulled myself up to the cable crossing and tightroped over the roiling creek, and if I had shouted I could not have made myself heard over the water's roar. In the bad drought year I prayed for this, the violence of rain, to be alone in the wilderness when everything came crashing down.

5.

Who will stand witness to the miracles of our time? Who will tell of the workers who loomed sheets, spindled thread, edged the millions of towels that once dried dinner dishes and damp bodies all over the world? The mill workers learn to drive postal routes, serve coffee and fried eggs, restock shelves at the discount store. Or they look for work and cannot find it, and when their socks wear thin they darn them, and when the patches wear through they tear the fabric into strips, knot strips into rope, stitch rope into rugs. They move in with relatives. They halve dosages, stop subscriptions, fix beans. Boil a bone, make a soup. Make things last. And some nights, to save electricity, they sit in the dark, as my grandfather used to. He sat on the old brown davenport as night fell, and would not light the lamp. Like him they sit in the dark, figuring, wrapping themselves in hard hope.

In a faithless time I have gone to the desert and seen there ocotillo, devil's buggy whip, naked canes rising from the stony ground. Gray, stippled with thorns, it rattled in the wind, and no plant has ever looked so dead to me. But I've seen, too, the desert after rain, when the ocotillo's tips force out petals red as any cosseted rose. The ocotillo plays at death, crying a song to the cold desert wind; the ocotillo in bloom is a god's hair ablaze with fire, or blood.

This was my vision: Go to the tulip tree in the depth of the bad drought year, carrying a pick if you can find one, or a sharp stone, or a spade. Clear the fallen leaves. Bear down on the spade until your arch blisters. Dig a trench in the brick-hard clay. Take off your shoes; bury them there. Cover them with earth. Tamp it down. Leave your bare footprints, dancing.

The night after I did this, clouds gathered and flung down rain. The drought broke as the Baptists, the Methodists, the Presbyterians had all prayed; as I had. Then I went to the place on the mountain's flank where bright water poured from a jutting pipe. People fill their jugs there, say that water heals, those minerals build bone. Where granite gleamed with wet and moss sparkled with mist, where water gushed from a dark stub, I cupped my hands and drank. I buried my shoes at the foot of a mountain tree. Let its roots, well watered, twine around those rusting buckles; let rain crumble that old metal into strength.

6.

A break in the battle: not a truce, but a pause during which both sides admitted exhaustion. The factions retreated—David and his men into the cave of Adullam, his enemy into Rephaim

Valley. The late sun shone red on the wall of David's cave. The men kindled fires of dried dung and thorny branches, husbanding the scarce wood; they scrubbed their blood-caked bodies and swords with sand, roasted a snared goat and ate of it, gulped their rationed water. The watchmen took their places. The others, weary unto collapse, unrolled their mats but would not lie down before David.

He sat on the dusty cave floor, staring at the dwindling fire. Something about fire can make a man nostalgic. Perhaps he thought of how he came to fight his first battle. He had gone to the encampment on an errand, taking provisions to his brothers; he had been a boy then, and eager. He was sick of his town, knowing every dwelling and rut in the road, how the marketplace smelled of sour milk and the tannery. He walked out the gate with a cloth-wrapped bundle: cheese to bribe the commander, bread his mother had baked, a bag of dates for her favorite son. How well she had known the commander and what he would demand. But when David arrived at the encampment the tents were filled with the groaning wounded, and the place resounded with the enemy's daily taunts. He had not had time for homesickness; that would come later, when even the stars and sky seemed different than they had when he lay in the field, surrounded by his father's herds, insulated from dew by a blanket his mother had woven for him.

Would that I could drink the water of the well of Bethlehem! he said, suddenly, startling the men from reverie. *To taste once more those sweet waters.* The others nodded their heads gravely, keeping their eyes on the fire, looking at him and then at each other. And to each other their eyes asked, *Is this a test?* But he did not see their glance, and gazed at the fire a long time before stretching out on his blanket. Soon he was sleeping the heavy, silent sleep of the career soldier.

They were three, even then his most trusted, those permitted to rest near him. But that night they did not sleep. Smothering the fire with sand, they passed the guards with a silent nod, picked their careful way down the canyon, and ran a looping oxbow around the enemy camp, their sandals' slap the only sound. The sleeping town of Bethlehem was strange with the presence of invaders. No snores or muffled love-cries came from the cloth-draped windows; no dog shambled down the street. Clay ovens ticked in the cool midnight air. Did they silence the enemy guards with their swords? Did they glide past so skillfully, keeping to the dark places between houses, that no one detected them? Somehow they made their way to the well, lifted the heavy lid that dripped with condensation, and hauled up the bucket. Did they drink? They had no time; wrapping the jar in a worn tunic, they turned to go. The moon sank as they ran across the desert, and they were keenly aware of every stone's shadow that could hide a man, every gully where a spy might crouch. Would they have heard the whicker of an arrow over the pounding of their breath? Would they have noticed if one of their group fell? The sky lightened as they ran into their own camp. They waited outside the cave until he rose.

Where have you been this night? he asked. *I heard the three of you rise and run down the canyon path.* His face was weary; he looked like someone who, a betrayer himself, knows he will never be able to trust another. One of the three pulled a bundle from his side, unwrapped a cloth, and held up a jar. *Water from the well of Bethlehem,* he said, sat down, feet still dusty, shins thorn scratched. David held the jar as though it were a serpent that might strike if not carefully handled.

Stand up, he said. Taking each man's face in his hands, he pressed his mouth to their stubbled cheeks. *I cannot drink this,* he said. *This could as well be your blood, my men, you who risked your lives for my pleasure.* The sun rose over the edge of the desert, and in the valley below, the enemy girded for battle. David fell to his knees, holding the jar to his chest, and the men instinctively put out their hands, shielding the vessel from harm. He raised his hands above his head and brought the jar crashing to the ground. The water seeped into the dry sand. *This is my offering to the God of Israel,* he said. *This blood of my men, these waters of my home.* Clay shards shiny with water, and the sun already drying them. The dark patch shrank, lightened, disappeared.

After that morning they were good as betrothed, David and his men, filial and pledged, they who would make together a history to be remembered long after their passing. They risked their lives to slake his thirst; they carried his home in a jar. He poured it out, the only use worthy of a holy thing. Did this offering please his God? The sun licked up the water, and it rose invisibly on its long journey, gone as though it had never been, until clouds gathered over the desert and dropped down rain. For water is a thing used hard, and used again; water is older than the bodies it laves, a relic scrubbed by charcoal and root, sparkling still as on its first bright day. Thousands of years later, the story survives; can't you see the cup outpoured? Can it be that even now, at this late hour, the very blood that swells your veins carries something of the waters of Bethlehem?

Everything but Your Wits

"And I followed her to the station / with a suitcase in my hand"

"Love in Vain," Robert Johnson, 1938

Station

The pump brays as someone works the enameled handle, a grip heavy and cool, marked with duller places from the oils of many palms. Then water stutters from the iron spout, and travelers step forward, canteens in hand. Children squeal as the cold water splashes them. Water puddles on the concrete.

Imagine a place filled with waiting people. They stitch patches to frayed pant legs, swap stories, smear lard on cracked sandals. Every now and then, a latecomer steps onstage and attaches to a group. Over there is someone stretched full length on the sand (or bench, or low-pile patterned carpet), catching a few winks. Gather your strength while you can.

So: the singing pump, the low hum of conversation, light snoring, dripping water. And a clicking, as from shuffling a stiff deck of cards, emanating from a large ebony *Departures* sign. It hangs in a conspicuous place, and the travelers glance up at it before turning back to their different tasks. Occasionally, after such a glance, a group jumps to its feet, collecting its knapsacks and bedrolls, and rushes off to some platform or trailhead. The purring click of the sign fires the travelers' blood. Bikers bound for the mountains pass around a tire pump, a roll of red grip tape. The travelers jig with excitement. Then a whistle blows, and they hurry to their respective gates.

Gate/Platform 1: Matamoros, Mexico

I dropped my quarter in the slot, and the turnstile gears clicked. A man launched himself toward me, saying *what is it you want, I help you.* I kept my eyes down. Under a warped ramada, a man played an upright bass with dark strings worn down, in places, to nylon white as a finger bone. Behind a plate glass window, meat roasted over glowing charcoal, the animal splayed on a rod, legs spread wide, muscles dry and purple red, revealing the twin ditches of its rib cage.

Then she appeared, a natural on high heels, pulled through the crowd by her father. It was her *quinceañera,* and the hem of her lavender gown flounced around her nylon-covered ankles. Dark curls, shiny with pomade, clung stiffly to her smooth temples. If that's what it was to be queen for a day, it wasn't anything she hadn't practiced, nothing she was scared of. So what if she was late for the party? They couldn't start without her.

Border-town girl, fifteen that long-ago day in July, I remember your poise, the flame your eyes held. Let men hurry; time is not your master. You vanished around the corner, past the taxi stand, but when I close my eyes I see you.

Gate/Platform 2: Tucson

The car seemed to come out of nowhere, a black Nova, glass packs so loud we suddenly had to shout. Once it roared past, four things in quick succession: I felt a sudden, sharp pain; the boys in the Nova shouted something out the window; an egg, stone hard, bounced off my side; it smashed on the sidewalk. Then the Nova was gone, blasting off into the night, taillights streaming red. Yolk smeared the concrete yellow. I thought: at least it wasn't a rock, at least it wasn't a bullet. The purple bruise below my rib cage faded to green, then yellow, and after ten days was gone.

Gate/Platform 3: Murrell's Inlet, South Carolina

She might have been thirteen, the girl on the bicycle, pedaling up and down Schooner Court all day long. Heavy, her hair in a lank ponytail, she kept her head down over the handlebars, and her blue shorts were dark with sweat. In mid-July, a mile from the beach—where those looking to economize stay—there's not much of a breeze. The early morning air is like a damp towel, and by noon, people who aren't used to the heat have a hard time catching their breath. In the evening the mosquitoes whine, the air smells like gunpowder from the fireworks, and little frogs make regular, taut calls, like car alarms. All that long day, the tires of her red bike hissed on the asphalt. No breeze rattled the palmetto fronds; the marsh air was thick enough to spoon, like custard. What did she think about, the girl on the bicycle? Once I think she saw me, sitting on the porch with a sweating drink in my hand, watching her. She just kept going, and as the sky got dark and the streetlights flickered on, I caught a snatch of the song she whistled: "Embraceable You."

Gate/Platform 4: Siracusa, Sicily

Their aim was very bad; the slanting rain got in their way, and the chain-link fence. But they were determined and resourceful, focused as children can be. One found a stone; the others slung mud. The women, tending braziers of coals that smoked in the rain, ignored them. I had passed their camp on my way to a fountain in Siracusa where, according to legend, you can drop a flower and later it'll surface in Greece. But when I found the fountain I'd forgotten to buy a flower; my heart wasn't in it. I leaned over the pool's edge and looked at the rain-dimpled water. Everything was gray, the stones lining the well, the streets, the old palazzi turned into storefronts selling gloves and copper cookware. I took a different way back to the train station; someone in the street showed me how. I'm sure those children—adults by now—forgot me by the time the sun set. What did I look like to them, a dripping girl with a back-pack and a broken umbrella? They hated me; their eyes burned with it.

Gate/Platform 5: Main Street

Savor the melancholy that comes from driving through a strange town after dark. It doesn't even have to be late; once the stores have shut down for the day, their display windows burn like stage sets under fluorescent lights. Notice the hard-ware store with cans of paint in its window, an assortment of beveled mirrors, canning jars. Signs read *We Sharpen Everything But Your Wits: Carbide Blades, Skates. Glass Cut. Custom Framing Available.* Pause there until the traffic light changes, then touch the gas. You don't belong here. By the time the workday starts again, you'll be long gone.

Gate/Platform 6: Terlingua, Texas

No shade nor scrap of green as far as the eye could see, and the sun bore down like a hammerhead. Rusty barbed wire edged the old graveyard. I walked slowly down the rows, sweating and reading the faded names, thinking of the well-watered city cemetery where I worked once, its green grounds studded with granite monuments polished to glass and gracefully lettered. Nothing like that here. The mourners' own hands had painted the names on the wooden monuments, piled stones at head and foot, smeared mortar between bricks. They filled the altars they had built with silk flowers, bottles of beer, and votives, spent now, tufts of blackened wicks at their bottoms. They must have dug the very graves, and what would that take in country like this? A whole day of swinging a pickaxe, stony chips flying, denting ground hard enough to twist metal. They did it them-selves, those mourners; they paid no one, laying their lost ones away instead watered with their own labors' sweat, heralded with their own bodies' hurt. That work had hallowed the red dust under my feet. A wooden tablet ringed with stones (violet, chalk blue, paprika) read, "In the arms of my beloved desert, know I am at rest."

GATE/PLATFORM 7: PUMPVILLE

Seemed like the wind always blew in west Texas, rubbing paint from the boarded-up storefronts, making the faded signs creak and bang. In a plate glass window, a menu yellowed, and an empty trailer hulked by the dry riverbed. I turned the car radio to "scan," and it riffed through empty air, picking up static. I listened for hours. There was no shade; there were no churches, and the only shadows were those cast by cinder-block buildings built by men who had left long ago. An old sign read "Hang Your Hat in Sanderson." When I drove through the next year, the sign was gone.

GATE/PLATFORM 8: EASLEY, SOUTH CAROLINA

The passenger train used to run through Easley at 10:42 every night. I worked at the movie theater then, and by that point in the evening I'd be sweeping up outside, emptying the urn of cigarette butts, beating dust from doormats. From the theaters came the muffled sounds of scripted mayhem—tanker explosions, percussive laughter. I brushed grit off the sidewalk under the humming sodium floodlight. It was a pensive time. And then the Klaxon of the passenger train. I leaned on my broom and watched the train approach, its headlight burning brighter as it rounded the curve. The train's wheels clicked, one-two, one-two, and across Highway 123 I saw passenger car windows, some lit, flash by. I wondered about the people on the train, where they were going, if they felt the excitement I did, whether any of them looked out their windows at the town, my town, that must have looked nondescript, to them. They would not know the story of the boarded-up textile mill, would not have gone to a funeral at the cemetery by the tracks (pale headstones sliding by in the dark), would not have stopped at the ice cream parlor for supper every Sunday after evening service, would not have tilted high above the tired crowd in the rickety Ferris wheel, set up by the tracks every Fourth of July, looking toward the dark place in the west where invisible mountains bunched.

GATE/PLATFORM 9: IOWA

On the Fourth of July, I dreamed a soldier. Walking a highway shoulder, his back to me, he wore a green uniform and carried a duffel. The material of his jacket stretched taut between his shoulder blades. This was corn country, and I saw waves of green plants, tall on the ridges, stunted and yellow in the low places where rainwater had stood. *Knee high by the Fourth,* we used to say. Every now and then, he bent to pick up a stone. He'd carry it a little while, then drop it, pick up another. One at a time. He looked solid, corporeal, his dark shadow moving over the gravel, but he was dead, I knew. He walked inexorably towards home.

Building a Funeral

In Houston, in June, the morning air shudders like set gelatin. Swamp water saturates the air; seen through it, everything takes on a greenish cast. As in all jungles, plants grow ferociously: banana trees, marsh grass, potato vines twirling overnight up guy wires, river cane. If all the people left, plants would take the place in six months flat. Texas heat is, of course, legendary. Believe all you have heard. Blacktop goes gummy; during a Dallas heat wave, the Department of Transportation closes a freeway because eighteen-wheelers rip up the asphalt with their heavy tires.

Houston is a sprawling city with an area greater than that of Rhode Island. As a resident, you can choose to be proud of this or not. In 1999, it's my first summer here, so I'm trying to decide. I prowl the city's ragged margins looking for work: singing waitress, journeyman carpenter, Gallup pollster, street sweeper, bikini car-washer, Tarot-card reader, Harley-Davidson seller. No takers. Downtown, Enron thrives, and pundits natter about "the new economy." The boldest predict that the Dow will never drop below ten thousand. Bull or bear, it doesn't much matter, because I am broke. I can't find a job anywhere. And then, in the classifieds of the *Houston Press*, I see the ad:

**Everybody
Needs It!
Cemetery Sales**

■ ■ ■

> If the prospect says, "I'm not interested," smile and
> agree with the feeling and say, "That's O.K.; you know,
> I don't think I know anyone that's interested in a ceme-
> tery. But since I'm already here, the best service I can
> give to you is to go ahead and issue this discount certifi-
> cate and be on my way. May I step in?"
>
> PRESENTATION SCRIPT, HOLLYWOOD CEMETERY

During training week, I learn about "pre-need" sales, visiting
potential customers in their homes and trying to sell property (plots or mausoleum space), caskets, concrete vaults, and
monuments. We don't have a funeral home, so all embalming
is done elsewhere; we take over at the actual graveside. My
manager, Richard Carlo, is a seasoned veteran of the death care
business—of which Houston is an international hub—as well
as a former postman and paratrooper with the name of his di-
vision tattooed on his beefy forearm. We spend hours in the
break room of the cemetery's office, going over our presentation script.

"People don't like to think about dying," he says. "Get them
used to the idea. You've got to take them out of denial if you
want to move property."

He flips to the next page of the *Why Pre-Plan?* section, a
photo of a teary woman in a black blouse. "Stress to the families
that pre-planning sends a message of love to those left behind,"
he tells me. "It says to them, 'I love you and I don't want you to
have to make these decisions alone.'" The woman in the photo
looks tired, in need of a comforting shoulder, a drink, a make-
over. If only she'd pre-planned. "Why should so many widows
be compelled to make these decisions alone?" reads the caption.
Much of the sales pitch directly targets women, though nobody
admits it.

"Don't call them 'graves,'" Richard says. "I don't like that
word. Try to take the dark cloud out of pre-planning—call

them 'ground spaces.' But for now, push mausoleum spaces."
The new mausoleum was supposed to be finished months ago,
and one of the groundskeepers lets me in on why it's not done
yet. The contractor didn't pay his workers, so they got frustrated
and hocked all of his equipment at the Fiesta Pawn across the
street. He went bankrupt, and the cemetery owners haven't
found a new contractor. The skeleton frame of the mausoleum
stands empty all summer, its concrete foundation littered with
construction detritus: lumber scraps, bent nails, empty bottles.

"It'll have six levels: the floor level, A, we call 'prayer level,'
B is 'heart,' and C is 'eye.' D through F are the cheapest levels," Richard says. "We call those the 'heaven' levels. Probably
as close to heaven as you're going to get," he says. He laughs,
and I understand that this laugh is something customers never
hear, are not supposed to hear. He is being himself, not a sales-
man; he has let me into his group. I am torn between distrust
and a desire to return his friendship, if that's what this is.

"Make sure to remind your customers that we're a perpetual-
care cemetery," he says, all business. "'Perpetual,' meaning
'forever.'"

▓ ▓ ▓

> Knock briskly six times (do not ring the doorbell),
> stand to the right center of the door and say: "Good
> evening, Mr. (or Mrs.) _____ (emphasize their name
> as though you know them). Fine, I am _____ (your
> name). May I step in?" At this time step to the left, wipe
> your feet, and enter the home.
>
> PRESENTATION SCRIPT, HOLLYWOOD CEMETERY

First thing next morning, the secretary says "So, you're going
to go selling plots door-to-door?" I think she's kidding, but
Richard doesn't laugh.

"Well, yeah, some of the salespeople actually do case the neighborhoods," he says. This is not something he mentioned in our phone interview. "But you have to have strong Spanish skills to be really successful at that. Our target market is typically Hispanic, mid-forties or older, lower to middle income.

"So I'm not going to send you door-to-door, Joni, but I do think you're ready for an in-home presentation," he says. "I'll go with you."

▪ ▪ ▪

There's a drift of candy wrappers and old newspapers in a corner of the chain-link fence, a gutted washing machine on the curb. A patchy dog bays at us. A woman emerges from the open garage, and Richard says, brightly, "Hello, my name is—"

"Are you the cemetery man?" she asks. "Come on in."

Her kitchen stinks of garbage and backed-up drains, and I am ashamed of myself for noticing this, for noticing the chinks in the wall where the window frames gap, for pitying the circumstances of her life even as she plans her funeral. She might be thirty-five. It's hard to tell.

Richard does most of the talking, and he does it by the book. He asks The Question that Always Makes You Look Good: "Have you ever had to make final arrangements for a loved one?" ("If the prospect says 'no,' emphasize how lucky she has been. If she says 'yes,' remind her of how traumatic those decisions were. Does she want that for her husband, her daughter, her son?") He shows her the list of "Forty-nine Things You Must Do on the Most Difficult Day of Your Life" (1. Call the coroner 9. Notify pallbearers 14. Provide vital statistics about the Deceased 25. Decide on casket 40. Pay for interment). I hold the presentation book, make eye contact, try not to think about it too much.

She decides on two plots in the Memorial Park ("Our Lady of Guadalupe") section of the cemetery, near the statue of Jesus Praying in the Garden. Memorial Park is the "most economical section," as well as the one directly targeted toward Hispanics. Richard told me earlier why these plots cost less: "The bayou, Little White Oak, borders this part of the property, and when it rains too hard, it floods. Remember the big storm last fall?" I did. Semis floated down I-10. "Bayou overflowed. Had water clear up to Jesus' chin."

We work out a payment plan, twenty dollars a month for the next six years, and she signs the contract. As we drive away, I ask Richard why he didn't tell her about the flooding problem.

"Look, we gave her a good discount on those plots, didn't we?" he says. "You saw how she lived. She's a grocery checker, she can't afford anything better than that. Now she's covered.

"You can't tell them everything," he says.

▦ ▦ ▦

"I sold a family plot in Memorial Park once," Dale tells me. He is Hollywood's top seller, fabulously good-looking, an aspiring model with the head shots to prove it.

"Yeah, so this family had a boy who drowned," he says. "I sold them that space at-need, plus eleven others on payments. They came to visit their son's grave after a big storm, and it was under ten feet of water. Man, were they hot. They wouldn't even talk to me. We had to dig up their son and bury him on higher ground."

▦ ▦ ▦

Two telemarketers cold-call people and give us a list of the ones who don't hang up. As a "Pre-Need Sales Counselor"— now that I've finished training, I have a title—I'm supposed to call these potential customers and set up sales appointments with them in their homes. So I do it, I call them, and I'm surprised at how few of them yell at me. If I were on the other end of the line, I think I'd resent that bright voice reminding me of my own mortality—and would I like to beat inflation by buying at today's prices?

I don't get many appointments. Richard tells me I need to push people harder. "You've got to remind them that they need it," he says.

▩ ▩ ▩

> (A Memorial) should not reflect sorrow but rather the long years of warmth and affection typical of the American Family.... As an essential part of our American way of life, a Memorial should speak out as a voice from yesterday and today to ages yet unborn.
>
> "What Is a Memorial?"

Between phone calls and house visits, I read up on monument literature. Monument lit is a genre unto itself; like most propaganda, riddled with wild promises, but peculiarly awful in its pledge to ease the sting of death while providing a measure of immortality. The balm of Gilead, they would have you believe, is made of good Georgia granite. It doesn't help that the retail price (as per Hollywood policy) is a whopping 385 percent of wholesale. What this means is that a modest headstone runs about one thousand dollars, and that's just in gray granite; Black Mist or Red doubles the price. A marker for two often totals three thousand, plus engraving.

So, if you're buying a monument—perhaps one from the "Rock of Ages" product line—what can you expect from your considerable investment? Royal Melrose Granites offers a headstone in Sunset Red, with a "delicately carved acanthus leaf, timeless symbol for the Garden of Heaven." The ad promises that "the strength of the solid granite design offers comfort and peace." Maybe it's possible to ease your pain with a nice slab of granite; people find comfort in surprising ways. But I don't buy it, not even the more tangible "strength" and "solid." Hollywood is littered with cracked monuments, victims of the groundskeeper's manic riding-mower runs.

I study lists of flowers and their meanings: iris for "elo-
quence and divine message," pansy for "thoughtful recollection,"
oak leaves for "virtue, stability, and faith." I want iris to be iris
and oak to be *Quercus,* deciduous, bearer of squirrel mast and
lender of shade. I want to gag. Only thistle carries a whiff of
humanity's honest stink: "a symbol of austerity, independence,
and earthly sorrow."

Nobody I know is buried in this cemetery. This makes a
difference. Here in Houston, I live my life in present and future only; without death, the past has no teeth. And so I walk
between the graves—part of my job—and read inscriptions
of my unknown dead. Many of them move me, particularly
those in Babyland. But of all the monuments, the one that
comforts me—about my life and my job in this place, a place
that is already starting to get to me—belongs to Fritz Hahn,
Houston blacksmith, 1898–1935. His headstone is an anvil. The
hollows he pounded are still there, and I rub them with the
heel of my hand. The cemetery is not without inhabitants. A
yellow-crowned night heron (breeding phase) stalks delicately
through a mud puddle. Masses of tadpoles shudder. There's an
alligator in Little Oak Bayou; he slinks away when we get too
close. *I have never seen anything this clearly,* I think. I allow myself to hope.

▪ ▪ ▪

People leave things at the cemetery. One day, while showing
spaces to a pair of prospective customers, Dale spots a plastic bag behind a bush. He doesn't mention it, but the wife
notices.

"The bag had a dead chicken in it," Dale tells me later. "She
yelled so loud, I thought she was gonna bust herself. Someone'd
cut the chicken's throat, so it was all blood and feathers, and
underneath was a bunch of bloody clothes. It turned out for the
best, though; I got them to buy mausoleum space instead."

Mysterious things: one morning, I find a red snapper, a pink votive, and a carnation on the grave of a woman who died in 1917. Bluebottles swarm the fish's empty eye. An enormous grackle perches on a nearby headstone, a rattling squawk coming from deep inside his chest.

I'm not sure what to make of these gifts—Dale calls them voodoo—but some of the other, less cryptic offerings move me. An unopened bottle of Corona. The plastic figures of jungle animals glued to a tiny marker in Babyland. A limp Mylar balloon that reads "You're So Special." A warped, rained-on *Feliz Cumpleaños* card, the kind that plays a song. From across the graveyard, I hear its tinny snatches of music, and finally figure out where it's coming from. She had been eighteen years old, and beautiful. The locket on her headstone was propped open so everyone could see her.

▨ ▨ ▨

After a couple of weeks, Richard pulls me into his office and asks me to switch from pre-need to at-need sales. This means that when someone dies, my phone will ring. I worry about getting emotional when confronted with the Recently Bereaved; I worry more about paying my rent, due soon, and figure at least I won't have to convince people that they need the plot. I take the job. The first thing I learn to do is wait. Between the many small but weighty events that make a graveside service, there are vacant hours. I find things to occupy my time.

▨ ▨ ▨

YOU ARE NOT LOCKED IN: ESCAPE DEVICE
Press the button.
Turn the handle.
Push the door open.

ROUND STICKER ON THE INSIDE
OF THE VAULT IN THE RESEARCH ROOM

Women, they're almost always women, usually in groups of two or three, and undoubtedly packing a notebook. Amateur genealogists have distinctive field markings. After a couple of weeks here, I can spot them at fifty paces.

By Houston standards, Hollywood is an old cemetery, with the first burial in 1895 (July 12, boy, ten months). So a lot of people trying to fill their charts come here for information. The Research Room is off-limits to them—exclusive as the stacks at Harvard—but not to me. They wait, more or less patiently, on the stained loveseat in the lobby while I look for their dead relatives.

Like Houston, the Research Room is outdated and hard to use, with a logic wholly its own: outsiders, beware. The central relic is a four-foot-tall Rolodex comprised of crimped metal pages that slap together when I turn it. All burials from 1895 through 1980 are listed here, each name typed on a thin strip of balsa wood that looks a lot like a coffee stirrer. A number next to each name corresponds to one of eight clothbound ledgers stacked on a sagging shelf.

One slow afternoon, I leaf through the ledgers, reading the fragments of lives taped to the crumbling pages. In a spidery hand, a woman's will, dated 1916. A letter typed in 1979, one sister refusing another burial in the family plot, "inasmuch as she had our brother disinterred and moved against his own wishes." A letter mailed during the Depression: "July 26, 1934, Kingsbury, Texas. We are all well but not prosperous."

One of my long-ago predecessors had filled the *Cause of Death* column with notes in a curling, long-extinct script. 1898 2 January, Thrown from Buggy. Congestion Chill. Black Jaundice. Chills of Fever. Locked Bowels. 1902 30 July, Killed in R.R. Collision Near Shreveport. Shot Self while Hunting. Found Dead in Hotel. I total the number of burials for each year. 1944 had been a big one—708, more than double that of 1943. "War Dead Shipped from France" appears, but in a different hand.

▦ ▦ ▦

The phone rings. It is the undertaker, telling us when to expect the family. Waiting for the next of kin is a nervous business. I want to get my part right, to press the hand with the right blend of compassion and confidence, to pass the correct props (contract, pen, Kleenex), to watch my cues, to defer. I believe they will notice if I get it wrong. It's certainly possible that I overestimate my role.

▪ ▪ ▪

Two children, a boy and a girl, sit in the waiting room. She giggles and he shushes her. The room is furnished with a dingy pair of couches, a crooked gold-framed mirror, and a coffee table laid with a bowl of potpourri and an enormous Bible open to John 14–17. The girl slurps a soda and stage-whispers in Spanish. A pair of plastic "bronze" roses, the kind sold as an accessory to grave markers, are thumbtacked to the wall. White-painted burglar bars are bolted to both the inside and outside of the windows. Outside, a Peterbilt idles at the red light, making the windowpanes rattle. I will never be able to smell this particular blend of potpourri without being transported back to this waiting room, this maroon carpet, this stagnant afternoon. Mary the secretary plays oldies in her office: Monkees, Beach Boys. The kids on the sofa pay no mind.

▪ ▪ ▪

Night falls. I go home and make the mistake of turning on the local news. I can't decide whether Channel 13's evening anchorman is companionable, depressing, or just familiar. The bad news never quits: someone finds a dead baby in a Dumpster, another knifes a guy for his station wagon, a boy shoots his cousin. It's a familiar story—two kids playing with a gun they think is unloaded. "How many times does this have to happen?" I ask the newscaster.

Next morning, the phone rings. I have an at-need.

▪ ▪ ▪

The mother doesn't say much. Her sisters take care of the forms, the signatures, the money. I can't look at her. I cannot help her, I know; it is enough that I do no harm.

"Will we have to pay for everything right now?" one sister asks, "or can we do a payment plan?"

"Well, we only allow payments on pre-need packages," I say, hiding behind the euphemisms. "When it's at-need, the company requires payment in full."

"What's *at-need*?" she asks.

"It means we need it *right now*," sobs the mother.

Later, we walk the narrow road to the space together. I hold the lot book and look away when they cry. A pine tree and the shadow of a pine tree. He was eleven years old. The service will be Tuesday.

※ ※ ※

Texas born, Texas bred,
When I die I'll be Texas dead.

DAN RATHER, ON *THE TONIGHT SHOW*, JUNE 22, 1999

The evenings are long, but I fill them. I walk aimlessly, read Eudora Welty, paint a picture of the *Titanic* from a kit. I string pearl-colored beads on dental floss. Pearls = Respectability. I call my mother. She tells me that Lou Holtz used to sell graves too. "'You've never sold anything!' his wife said. That summer, he sold their furniture, their refrigerator, and their washing machine." This is the punch line. I brood.

Outside, in the yard below my apartment, a possum noses around a bowl of soggy cat chow. The backs of his pink paws are covered in dark fur; he is wearing black fingerless gloves, very natty, like Cyndi Lauper. Now, past midnight, the sky is a bright pink-orange, Red Lake #40. A Norway rat runs along a power line. He is silent, lean, and speedy. The constant surf of traffic on 59. Thrumming sodium lights.

I go inside and lie on the stripped bed, planning an escape, thinking *toothbrush, penknife, King James Version, gas money*. I pack and repack my bags until morning comes.

▪ ▪ ▪

Tuesday. I iron a black dress, polish my shoes, clip on my fake pearls, apply sunblock. I've been burned just walking to a site; how much worse will a service be? The tent, after all, is for family members; they're paying for it. I will stand aside, at a respectful distance.

When I get to the cemetery, I drive the route in my Camaro, entrance to gravesite, so when the procession arrives I can lead them without getting lost. I envision chilling scenarios: the car runs out of gas. I forget and leave the radio on, loud. I lead the procession down the wrong lane. There are no blind alleys—someone has thought of this—and the layout is basically a horseshoe with smaller loops tacked to it. Still, there is a "way" and a "better way." Who wants an excruciatingly slow drive-by of the maintenance shed, the broken monuments and stray shovels, the Dumpster with muddy silk flowers scattered out front?

What if the workmen forget to dig the grave? Instead of a deep, cool rectangle, its corners neatly squared, there will be two little red flags, that's all, two red flags flapping helplessly in the wind. I wait. I worry.

The caterwaul of a siren. Three o'clock: right on time. The procession pulls in, first the hearse—"rolling stock," undertakers call it, with more than a touch of pride—then the limos for the family, the everyday cars of the other mourners. I ease down Palm Drive at a respectful 12 mph, glancing in the rearview at the hearse behind me, making sure nobody gets left behind.

We arrive. The pallbearers, none of them out of high school, pull the child-sized casket (*Our Lady of Guadalupe*, #112, gas blue) from the hearse. A little boy of six or seven grabs one of the silver carrying bars. He reminds me of a ring bearer.

The priest wastes no time; he's done in ten, censer jutting from his pocket like a mike. He shakes holy water over the casket and leaves. The undertaker grabs a pail of crumbly dirt, and as the mourners file past, each throws a pinch on the casket. Like Communion, everyone seems afraid to get too much.

All this takes a while; a line of mourners snakes down Palm Drive. Downy-legged girls, his nervous classmates, too young to shave. Serious men—his teachers. Neighbors, relatives, friends. The PTA sent a floral spray.

Mothers clutch their children. One woman stands behind her son the whole time, arms around his neck, face pressed to his nape. The mother of the dead child is expressionless, blanked by grief. The others, sympathetic, mourn too, but they don't want to share her place. The mothers hold their children until they squirm.

I stand aside. I am not supposed to take part in this grief. I am here in case of emergency, though what could be worse than what's already happened? I let my eyes go out of focus. I think about my work.

Once the corollary mourners leave, walking solemnly to their cars, I give the groundskeepers the signal. They have been smoking under a shade tree since the beginning of the service—at a respectful distance, of course, though I could still hear the rise and fall of their conversation. They walk over, pull the tarp off the dirt, and start dismantling the tent. The undertaker motions the pallbearers to move the casket to the grave, and Walter drives up in the big yellow backhoe.

They drop the casket onto the lowering bed. Antonio and José, done with the tent, unspool the strips holding the casket at ground level. One man for each end, they lean over the grave, rolling the bars of the bed until the casket hits the bottom of the concrete vault. Antonio climbs into the grave, pulls the spray of dahlias and gladiolus off of the casket, and boosts himself out. Members of the family stand in the patchy sunlight, watching Walter as he hooks the lid of the vault with the backhoe and maneuvers it into the hole. It lands with a loud chunk, concrete against concrete. The men of the family pick up the shovels Antonio gives them and go to work.

Most of them add one or two clods of dirt, then pass the shovel on, but one handsome boy of eighteen or twenty loosens his tie and keeps digging. It's not ceremonial; he wants to fill the grave. The shovel bites into the mound of dirt. He bears down on his loafer-clad foot, lifts his load, and throws it in the hole, violently. Time and again he does this. There's a rosebud stuck in his back pocket. His Adam's apple shakes as he fights back tears.

When the men have finished, Walter pulls the backhoe around and fills the grave completely. He concentrates intensely, as he always does. Not a crumb falls unintended. Not a stray flower does he crush. Finally he smooths the grave and tamps the dirt. The boy's parents leave. I hang around, picking up dropped cups and wads of Kleenex.

Antonio and José help me arrange the casket sprays around the fresh grave, and I take a Polaroid. ("Families like to have a picture of the grave looking all nice," Richard claims.) When the photo develops, the ribbons on the arrangements banked around the grave show up as blue blurs. There is no headstone; there has not been time to have one cut. In the background stands the Dumpster, full of construction trash from the mausoleum. Broken boards and chunks of concrete are strewn around. Downtown skyscrapers show as hazy square shadows. I take another shot from a different angle and run inside just ahead of the sudden cloudburst.

▩ ▩ ▩

There are the usual economies: reused foil, low-wattage bulbs, the careful laying by of leftovers. I scrimp on air conditioning; my apartment is a sweat lodge. Ninety degrees at midnight. In the closet, shoes sprout filaments of green mold. *Check #577, Houston Light and Power, $23.44, July Payment.*

After two pay periods come and go without a check, I find out the only thing we don't get paid for is at-need opening and closing—funerals, essentially, all I've been doing since I started. I can quit now and cut my losses, or stay and hope to sell a monument or two. I decide to stay. In the meantime, money is tight. I allow an occasional splurge: grated nutmeg for a meat-sauce recipe, an adventure-travel guide ("Biking across Vietnam"; "Rafting the Omo"; "Summiting Kilimanjaro"), gasoline.

Some nights I can't sleep, so I drive. The 610 Loop is my standby. Forty-two miles, and if it's late enough, I can ring the city in half an hour. I pass the Bud brewery, the flaming stacks of the Ship Channel, Port of Houston, AstroWorld's rickety coasters, Carmen's Secreto XXX Emporium, and the Transco Tower, whose lighthouse beam sweeps slowly over my city. I tell exits like beads. Some nights I can't make myself walk up the steps to that apartment, can't turn on the light and see it empty, can't face another night in that bed. So I drive too fast, and it is a drug. I drive the funerals and the death out of me and into the asphalt still warm from a long day. I hold it in. I keep going.

▓ ▓ ▓

The undertaker at one service whispers through the whole thing. "My family was a dynasty of Texas undertakers," he tells me. "Twenty-four of us in the business, and offices in San Antonio, Dallas, Houston, New Braunfels, Monterrey."

The thing that's different is his hands. The dark jacket, the forty extra pounds, the razor-parted hair—I expect. All summer, the undertakers I meet vary little from type. But the others have hands that are cool and fleshy; there are no bones inside them, but cartilage, like sharks. This man's palm is hard as an old boot, and his knuckles are big, like an assembly-line welder's, knobby from repeating the same motion thousands of times. He stands next to me, clasping those hands in front of him, whispering.

"Every person has ten friends," he says. "Conquer one, and you conquer their ten friends too. Give these people compassion and you'll tie them to you with a knot that won't break."

"I've got roots in this community," he says. "Deep roots in the soil. This year I expect to help four hundred families. There's a whole army behind me now."

▪ ▪ ▪

Morning. Someone must have made a good sale, because there's a box of Shipley's donuts on the break table next to an urn of cremains. I read the *Chronicle*, but not the obits. Old news by now. If there's business to be had, the phone will ring.

Dale walks in, eating breakfast on the run. Today, as always, he has a can of tuna, a protein shake, and a bowl of cold oatmeal; as always, he is in a hurry. He talks with his mouth full, never opens his tuna cans all the way. Time is money. As my grandfather used to say, "People are dying now that never died before."

"Got my head shots back," he says. And they're not bad: the Intellectual (Brooks Brothers button-down), the Soccer Star (bare chest, green shorts), the Man Reflecting (eyes closed, droplets of water on the lashes, pouting lip). The Many Moods of Dale. He's the crown prince of cemetery sales, Hollywood's top seller two years running, with the plaque to prove it. Glossy composite board with a tiny gold-plated shovel pegged to it. *Richard'll go around the bend if Dale ever leaves,* I think.

"Ever seen a grave probe?" he asks. "I need to find a space to bury a guy. You can come if you want."

Grave. Probe. These words should never be joined. But I'm curious, so I go along. The deal is done with a T-shaped bar six feet long. I don't know which is worse: hitting something, or not. We hit one. It must have been a newer burial, post-1970, after the cemetery started requiring vaults in order to prevent casket collapse. The older burials—1910, 1914, wooden caskets— we know they're there, but they're gone.

I find out later that some of the groundskeepers make extra money by selling stray bones the backhoe unearths. "Witch doctors grind them up for potions," Dale tells me, over the phone, after I've already left.

▓ ▓ ▓

The phone rings. The deceased had served in the Army between Korea and Vietnam. Forty years came and went. I shake hands with his two sons and arrange the service. Because he was a veteran, an honor guard will be there.

The members of the honor guard are older than I expect. The five of them arrive an hour before the service, cramped into the captain's red '91 Mustang; they need to set up. I tell them where the grave is and they head for it.

At first, it's the standard thing: the procession arrives and follows me back to the site (respectful 12 mph), the pallbearers unload the casket (flag draped), the priest says his thing and kisses his stole, an old woman sings a sad song. The honor guard stands at parade rest.

An enlistment-day photo rests on an easel near the casket. I try not to stare, but I do, and it's a mistake. Bright eyes, dark tonsure of hair, hopeful smile. He's so young, and so familiar; he looks a lot like my father, whose own enlistment photo hangs on a wall back home, in South Carolina. This picture is even faded in the same way, the whites turned yellow, the blacks and grays gone green. My father is alive, thank God, and I try not to think of him. I look away.

The song ends, and two members of the honor guard, the sagging captain and another, taller man, position themselves at either end of the casket. They start reading from cue cards; English now, though the rest of the service has been in Spanish. I lean against the glossy black quarter panel of the hearse. Distant thunder.

I will forget most of what these men read, as the other mourners will. That is all right. Part of why these uniformed men have come is to provide sound, noise, the semblance of companion-ship in an empty room. "Our ranks march on, one thinner," says the captain, and in the darkening gloom it's easy to imagine rank upon rank of marching soldiers. Uniforms pressed, eyes bright, they advance as one body, bathed in sepia light. We strain our ears for the sound of one slipping out of step, slumping to the ground. And we hear it, just as a coin dropped in a crowd turns heads: we hear what we listen for, what we value.

"Commander, present our nation's colors to the daughter of our fallen comrade," says the guard to the captain. They grasp the corners of the flag, lift it taut, and fold it in a tight triangle as the clouds break and the rain comes. The captain turns stiffly and paces to the deceased man's daughter. Her shoulders shake. He bends at the waist and places the flag on her lap, and she starts to sob.

Homily read, the captain and the guard trudge into the rain and join the other three next to the grave. "Commander, order twenty-one-gun salute to honor our fallen comrade," the guard says. Three of them snap to attention, as best they can, and shoulder their rifles. Click, boom, they shoot off one round of blanks. Three brass cartridges fall to the wet grass. Click, boom, another, another, until they've done seven rounds. And while they do this, it starts raining harder. Rain drums on the tent, splashes on the hood of the hearse, mingles with the crack of the guns and the sound of tight crying.

One of the guards breaks attention to hit "play" on a water-proof tape player set on a stand, and out comes a scratchy "Taps," barely audible over the spattering of the rain. When the song finishes, all five of the guards drop to their knees in the wet grass, fumbling for the spent cartridges. Rain runs down their freckled scalps and into their ears as they paw the ground, bits of sodden grass sticking to their fingers.

The captain collects the shells in a paper sack, which he gives to the daughter. The bottom of the bag leaks onto her lap. The others gather their rifles, their boom box, their stand,

and prepare to go. The short captain winks at me when he marches past. "See you next time," he says. That's when it gets to me.

I never knew this man. If he'd been younger, he might have known my dad, served with him in Vietnam, taken his picture at boot camp. Listen: my dad is okay. Today is his birthday—remarkable coincidence—and maybe right now, lunchtime, Mom is cutting a slice of carrot cake for him; maybe tonight they will go out to Steak and Ale. He is all right. And I—I am not sitting in that chair with a flag on my lap. It is not my time. Not yet.

But I cannot say any of this as I stand there in the rain, holding on to the old captain of the guard, my arms around his neck, sobbing into his shoulder.

"Let it out, honey," he says, "just let it out."

▪ ▪ ▪

I decide to leave. *Beat inflation; grieve in advance.* No more. I always put it in terms of those I know.

▪ ▪ ▪

Do not regret growing older. It is a privilege denied to many.

QUOTABLE DAY PLANNER, SEPT. 20. AUTHOR UNKNOWN.

The phone rings. A child, four years. The father arrives an hour later, and I take him into the room with the big round table where we sign the contracts. He has no money. He doesn't tell me this, doesn't have to. The one thing we are never to do is give discounts on at-need merchandise. Most things have two prices, pre- and at-need, with at-need generally higher; when you have a captive customer, it makes sense to capitalize.

"Look," I tell him, "this is what I can give you." I speak softly, so Richard won't overhear, and quote a price half of what it ought to be. He signs and leaves, and I give the copy of the contract to Richard.

"This is the price we're giving them," I say. What can he do, dock my nonexistent paycheck? "Dale will do their funeral. I'm leaving tomorrow for South Carolina; I'm going home."

What can he say? "Drive safe," he says, as he always does. I gather my things and go.

■ ■ ■

I hope no young woman plans my funeral. I want an old woman with a womb stretched from bearing or small, barren, fig-shrunk: empty. I want someone with small veins and slow blood, whose eyes will stay dry and open and whose mind will be on something else, preferably a grocery list or an unpaid bill. Some common thing of life. I want someone experienced in grief, who can put it on like a coat and hang it on a hook when it passes its time of use.

I want to tell her, Bury me head first, or not. Nobody will know the difference but you, and you'll forget by tomorrow, when your work day starts again and you do what you do: take the body from those who loved it living, keep it safe, play along. Do the best you can; do no harm. They will forget, have forgotten already, any kindness you may have done. This does not matter. Do what you can and hope that when your time comes, someone will do the same for you and for those who stand around the hole in the ground, looking in.

Postcards from Costa Rica

I.

Morning. An ant carries a scrap of green leaf above its head like a banner. When it meets another ant, its antennae play over the face of the newcomer, then it continues on its way. The quick cabal of touch. Another follows, and another, and I'm crouched down, hugging my knees to see better, following the leaf-cutters' line back to its beginning, a pile of snipped green wilting at the base of a tree. Ants troop down the trunk with bits of leaf on their backs, reach the ground, and follow the rest down the trail they've made, a lighter swath across the dark sand. At the trail's end, more ants disappear into the awl holes of nest, piles of excavated sand cresting the base. Underground, I know, they'll hang the leaves in chambers and feed on the fungus that grows there. How did they figure it out? Next morning, after a hard rain, the ants are at it again, pounding a new trail from tree to nest. But why this particular tree? Other trees, the same species, grow closer by, but the ants ignore them.

2.

The poppy-red sand crabs vanish at my lumbering approach, pouring themselves into their holes like a dose of medicine into a throat. If I'm still long enough, they'll venture out again, eventually ignoring me. On the tips of their legs they move in curving paths, stitching the damp sand with parallel strokes, twirling bits of sand into tiny spheres that dot the beach. From the taut sheet of beach they pick bits to pass between claw and mouthpart. Something tells them when to stop; all the balls of

sand are the same size. Inscrutable knitters, fraying and picking, loosening their strands from the whole, forever making
ready and never casting on.

3.

A crashing of leaves, whistling descent, and then, unmistakable,
landing's heavy thump. An iguana has fallen out of a tree. He
shakes his crested head, as if to clear it. He's long as my leg,
ankle to hip, a magnificent, gem-crusted creature; collecting
his wits, he slowly (gingerly?) puts one webbed foot in front of
the other and stalks away, though I've seen others run standing
when agitated. He leaves behind angled lines of claw marks,
and his dragging tail's shallow ditch. Now and then he'll stop,
to swallow green pods (seeds of a tree I can't identify), to bask
on the sand in the sun.

4.

Walking along the tide line, past midnight, I see a dark bank
of trees, the bright moon on the water. Punctures in the sand:
clam holes. A silently trotting dog. And then, two parallel tracks,
scalloped and smeared, each the width of a deck of cards, leading from the water to the upper reaches of beach. After a minute I recognize them, interpret the marks as something I've
hoped for years to see. I flick my light up the beach and there
she is, an olive ridley, come back to the beach of her birth to
bury her own eggs. There the hollowed pit, there the white egg
dropped. I turn the light off and she's invisible, and the sounds
she must be making—scraping sand, soft deposit—are wiped
clean by the crashing surf. Next morning there's another set
of tracks near the first, these leading back to the water. Where
the nest must be there's no other sign. Already, six a.m., the
sun warms the sand under my feet, the hidden young beneath
the sand.

5.

Morning. An open-air diner in a mountain village. I order *gallo pinto* (spotted rooster) and *café con leche,* then sit down to wait. Meanwhile, a woman does many things at once: washes a huge aluminum stockpot, relights the gas with a piece of paper after a gust blows it out, stirs a bubbling kettle of beans. Another woman cries out with joy when a child appears in the open doorway. Dressed in dark pants and a pressed white shirt, he carries a bag of books, ready for a day at school. After hugging him close she seats him at a table and gives him breakfast—beans and rice, eggs, a glass of juice. They talk quietly between bites. Soon he must leave, and she straightens his combed hair and adjusts his collar. Then, with one hand on his shoulder, her other plays over his face, and I can't tell what she's doing—crossing his forehead, his cheeks one by one, his chin, his red mouth. She could be brushing him clean, flicking away invisible crumbs, but the action's rapid and precise, prac- ticed looking, as though it stands for something. May no harm touch him. May his face stay always so bright. After he's gone she sits alone awhile, drinking her cup of coffee, before getting up to wash the dishes.

6.

Marks on a page, tracks and punctures and glyphs in the sand: these, my closest notes, I still can't translate, only squint and puzzle while the wind scours them clean. Years have passed and here's what I remember: a beloved child; the careful, constant work of insect, crustacean, reptile. I'll honor the glory of these days' passing, tell the things my eyes have seen.

The Rain Follows the Plow

> Between Burns and Bend lies the High Desert, grave-
> yard of homesteaders' hopes. When the better lands
> of Oregon had been taken up, land-hungry settlers
> swarmed into this, one of the most inhospitable regions
> of the continental U.S. High, arid, treeless, and chill, the
> country baffled the utmost labors of the homesteaders
> and destroyed their dream of a new wheat empire.
>
> OREGON: END OF THE TRAIL,
> *OREGON WRITERS' PROGRAM, WPA, 1940*

We know little about her, save that she took a 160-acre homestead under her name, alone.

JEFFERSON COUNTY, CENTRAL OREGON, 1911

She dreamed of drowning and woke to canvas snapping in dry
wind. She dreamed of swimming and woke to blankets damp
with sweat. She dreamed of draining the ocean and woke, her
mouth stitched into a dry pouch. She woke alone, morning
after morning, and once she dreamed he was beside her, warm
and solid, dreamed of him as he had been during their long
journey from home to here. Closer than that they had never
been. Dreamed his hips in the hollow of hers and as she woke
she felt him leave her, rising slowly, and all day thought she felt
the press of him, the gone ghost of what their bodies had been
together.

The sun rose early there, July in a high latitude, and that
morning she was up before dawn, her feet crushing dark lava

sand and scant dewfall. She picked her way down the trail to the place where three rivers met and hauled up buckets of water, her sunburned arms aching and sore. Two trips for the garden, one for herself. Then she set off for Culver.

The neighbors' child was watering the potato field by the time she passed. He walked slowly down the rows, carrying a bucket and a dipper with holes punched in it, parsing out the drops. He couldn't have been more than eight or nine, but serious already. Life out here could do that to a child. She kept going, heading east, to where the sun had cleared the horizon, a pale bright brand.

Going to town was not an errand she relished. The men stood in the shade, watching her, murmuring: *shameful, her claiming land out there by the Deschutes, when plenty of men with families need farms.* Ignoring the fact that most men, even those with brothers or children to help, couldn't make a crop off the scant eight or ten inches of rain that fell in a good year. *The river's nearby, yes, but tough to reach,* she thought, *an hour's hard hike by the time it's done, and what trail was there at the beginning of the summer? It's the weight of my feet that beat that path.* She stepped into the cool dark of the general store and chose a salted slab of pork from the rust-streaked barrel, ten pounds of flour, molasses. The shopkeeper measured a pound of nails into a hopper, poured them into a funnel of heavy kraft, and tied the bundle with twine, as careful with his words as the neighbor boy had been with his water. He had no personal enmity for this woman, nor those like her, but he'd heard the ranchers talk, cursing the recent influx of homesteaders who'd come to the area and the government that encouraged them. *Even when they come single, they don't come alone,* the ranchers liked to say. *They bring wire and fence posts, and what bunchgrass can a working man's cattle find, now that the country's sectioned off like this?* The shopkeeper totted up the price, counted her money, handed her change. She packed her leather bag with purchases—*look how she loads herself like a horse; what respectable woman would*—and turned to go.

A commotion outside as the Oregon Trunk line wheezed into town, metal wheels screaming to a halt. The innkeeper had ordered a cast-iron stove, and the men wrestled its crate off the boxcar, dropping it with a clang on the dusty roadbed. One of them wrenched the crate's lid free with a crowbar, nails yelping as they gave. She remembered the stove she had left back home, less than a year ago, and the scorch marks on her old plank floor. If she could get the field cleared soon, and rye prices were good—if she saved enough to buy a cow, and could sell butter and cream—someday, she would have a cookstove again.

She stopped at the blacksmith's to retrieve her spade; its flimsy metal had bent when she bore too hard against a buried stone. She paid the smith, gathered her things, and set off, the sun high by now. No onlooker spoke to her, a woman new-come, homesteading alone, out in the backcountry where the river ran swift and clear over the canyon floor.

Summer sunlight lasted long there, and she was grateful. She put Culver behind her and turned toward home, the mountains beside her still covered in snow no matter how the lowlands broiled, those mountains whose names she did not know: Three-Fingered Jack, Broken Top, and the Three Sisters—Faith, Hope, and Charity. From where she stood, the Cascades looked like the outline of a reclining woman, one breast erect against the reddish sky, and she wondered if this was a sign that she was truly lonesome, that even the landscape brought to mind a person. She had never been much of a talker—too much to do, even when her husband had been alive, and talk had not been their currency—but sometimes she could not remember the last conversation she'd had, and was surprised to find that she missed talk. So she spoke to herself. Who was there to hear? It hurt nothing, the indulgence of a woman, harmless. If the men in the shaded town could know that. She was a harmless woman, that was all. What could they have to fear from her? Silvery clumps of sage dotted the plains, and dark juniper staked meager shade. She could not vote in any election. Maybe it did not matter to her. She had no time to keep up with politics. Winter was coming.

It was better than eight miles from town to the river, and a hard climb from there to her camp. She laid her things away in the wagon bed, wrapping the food well for fear of animals, and spent the rest of the day clearing part of what she intended for her rye field. Sometimes she wondered if there would be any dirt left once all the rocks were gone. And yet she had heard that the soil here was rich, that you could grow anything in it if you could keep the young plants wet. The sun dipped toward the west, behind the mountains, as she worked. Fence lizards wriggled off the sun-warmed rocks and into clumps of sage; ants boiled out of sandy tunnels. Sweat ran down her back, dripped in the dust. She kept working until it was too dark to see, and Mars rose red above the horizon line. Her thumbnails were purple with blood where she had dropped stones on them. She fell into her pallet bed, asleep before she even said her prayers, and early in the morning, before dawn, yelping coyotes woke her, and she rose. Summer days were long but few. She could not afford to spend much more time clearing the field. The patch of potatoes she had planted would not be enough to last. She needed something to trade, rye, and for that she needed a cleared field; she worked without resting, and would not be stopped.

Green, who owned a nearby ranch he called The Cove, built his cabin out of Doug fir logs floated down the river in rafts. But he had the money to afford it, as well as other luxuries like the fruit stock, apple and peach, he planted in the bottomland. He was close to the river. Even as little boys, his sons had lugged buckets of water from the river to the orchard, he had told her, describing for her the saplings the trees had been, as they began to leaf out in their orderly rows. She had thought it the folly of an eccentric, but said nothing, gazing at the lines of spreading trees, growing into maturity now and carefully pruned, their trunks dark with damp. And just a few days after, one of

Green's boys had struggled up the trail to her camp, bearing two swollen apples, and she did not regret holding her tongue. Folly it had been and still was, but a man like Green could afford it. She could suffer an open-handed fool, devouring what he sent her.

Walking her claim that first morning after arriving—had it been only a few months ago?—she had known that she would have to find enough building materials to make something like a cabin before winter came. Money was scarce—almost all of their savings had gone to the doctors, useless, at the end—and so was wood, though she gathered what juniper she could grub with hoe and hands, stacking the tough branches in a pile. Rock was the only material she had plenty of, and she had to clear the fields anyway. Day after day she lugged rock into heaps, and every night she sank into sleep in the wagon, the canvas snapping in the wind that kicked up at sunset. She planned the cabin she would build of gathered stones. She would chink its holes with silt and sand, roof it with canvas from the wagon, weight the cloth with more stones and juniper branches, thatch it with bitterbrush. That would get her through. Meanwhile, when she was too tired to make another trip to the river, she took dust baths like a bird, the creases of her flesh dark with powdery earth. She rubbed her skin with sage leaves and chewed them for freshness. Back home, she remembered, she'd had a well. How wealthy she had been, and had not known it.

Water was the precious, powerful thing. It cut a hollow in the stone and cut it deeper, deeper, slicing the desert like a black-bottom pie and revealing what had happened before. Layers of ash after a volcanic eruption, and beneath that chunks of lava that had been slung out first, beneath that the smooth cobbles of a rocky river. The water kept cutting, and after a great storm or winter snowmelt from the high mountains it cut swiftly. Water keen and fast, or deliberate and heavy, water grinding and licking, polishing and knocking.

Sometimes rattlers coiled on the rock wall, sunning themselves. She shot the biggest ones through their wedged heads, sliced the skin open and pulled out pale vertebrae and yellow poison sacs. She fried the meat in a pan and ate it, burning the scraps so as not to attract cougar. The bones she dug a hole for and covered to keep away pain, an old habit she allowed herself. In this way she passed her first season, alone.

▪ ▪ ▪

Time passed, not much, ten years, twenty. Time enough for most of the homesteaders to pack up and leave, after the string of mild years ended and even the poor rains stopped. Some moved back east; some moved to Bend, working on the timber crews, and their descendants live there still, skiing Mount Bachelor in the winter, hiking The Sisters in the summer, living in the green shadow of the clear-cuts their grandsires made.

They left in a hurry, most of them, as if they'd hung on as long as they could, and when they finally gave in, they didn't have a minute to spare. They left pans hanging on hooks, seed catalogues on shelves, everything but the clothes on their backs and the food in their mouths. An example: a man rose early, lit a fire, and heated water for coffee. He sat at the table he'd made himself, drinking, as the sun rose in a red knot. Draining the dregs, he set the cup in its saucer, *plink,* then pushed away from the table and stepped out the door, as if going to check on something. He never returned. For years to come, travelers looked through the cabin's broken window and saw that coffee cup still sitting there, filling slowly with dust. The failed homesteader seemed doubly absent then for the homely thing he left behind, a cup of coffee long drunk, the rim his lips had pressed as his eyes looked over the bare room with its familiar constellations of knotholes, its every rough place planed.

Over the next ten years or so, most of the towns emptied. Men nailed planks over windows; stacks of mail piled on post-office floors. But some places hung on: Redmond, Metolius, Culver. In 1941, the state of Oregon bought out Green's descendants and turned The Cove and the surrounding ranch land into a state park. The Civilian Conservation Corps built superintendent's quarters, cabins, a workshop, and in the warm summers, a few travelers came. Twenty years passed. Northward, an afternoon's drive over improved roads, Portland grew, demanding more of everything, especially electricity. In the 1960s, hydroelectric was the going thing. Portland General Electric scouted the place where three rivers met—the Metolius, Crooked, and Deschutes—and decided to block the water with a great dam whose turbines would create energy for Portland. The resulting reservoir lake would inundate the state park there; PGE promised to build a new park on higher ground. The dam would eradicate the Metolius salmon by frustrating their migration; kokanee salmon, PGE countered, would flourish in the deep water. The dam project made its methodical way through the courts, and the electric company won. They settled on the name Lake Billy Chinook, after the Wasco scout who showed Kit Carson the area on an 1843 mapmaking expedition. Then, at the end of 1964, the rains came.

On a cold December morning, a gray day dawned. The boulders piled at the foot of the canyon cast no shadow, and the walls of basalt rising a sheer four hundred feet seemed painted with moisture. Green's ranch house, corral, and orchard still stood on the bank of the river. The place was deserted; there would be plenty of time, everyone thought, to salvage the lumber before the waters rose. And yet the day threatened rain, or seemed to. Then a fat drop fell.

The riverbanks were lined with pumice, volcanic stone so frothy with air that it bobbed like wood on water. A pale knob of pumice—nobody would have seen this—darkened as the raindrops, falling fast by now, soaked it. Puddles formed. As the rain continued steadily through the morning and into the afternoon, the puddles joined themselves to each other, and the pieces of pumice began to float on the shallow water. Night fell. By dawn, the river was swelling over its banks, licking at the tangled roots of the alder thicket and inching up their trunks, swallowing them and still rising, crawling up the dead juniper on the high ledge, and then straight up the canyon walls, four-hundred-foot cliffs cut with little shelves where chickweed and yarrow and hot rock penstemon grew in the summertime, drowning them. Pumice swirled in the current, floating high above what had recently been the riverbed. Still the rains came, drenching, heavy rains day after day, in this desert country lucky to get ten inches of rainfall a year. Portland General's engineers had estimated it would take a year for the lake to fill. It was done in a week, millions of gallons of water covering everything, stretching for miles along the new shoreline, creating the huge reservoir they called Lake Billy.

The rain follows the plow, the homesteaders used to say, and tried to believe it. Railroad and government brokers had lured them to the High Desert on the notion that farming dry land could cause climate change, that a person could induce rain to fall by needing it badly enough. The homesteaders found out the hard way that in central Oregon, the sun and rain kept their own counsel. But when the Christmas rains of 1964 came, it was as though the rain followed the dam, and the skies accompliced themselves to the work of drowning forever what used to be. Even Noah's God allowed forty days and forty nights; the rains swallowed the old ranches in one week's time.

■ ■ ■

THE COVE PALISADES STATE PARK, 2001

In the spring of 2001, I was finishing two master's theses, teaching undergraduates, and hunting summer work that would get me out of Houston for a while. City life wore hard on me. I'd worked as a park ranger in South Carolina the year before and decided to strike out for a new territory, hitting on Oregon almost by chance. I took a job at the Cove Palisades in central Oregon, a place I knew nothing about, despite the packet of local history the park superintendent sent me a few weeks prior to my departure. I would learn about that desert country, what and who had shaped it, but first I had to make the long haul from Texas to Oregon.

There was a man whose everything fired me—how he turned toward me when I spoke, the breadth of his hands, the dark hair curling at his temples. I thought his daily transactions marvelous. How a store clerk could hand him a receipt (feigning boredom!) I could not fathom. I loved words, had spliced myself to their lessons, but when he came near I could not think what to say.

On the Saturday before leaving, I was making ready, changing the car's oil and checking its tires, stashing dried fruit and jugs of water in the trunk, choosing field guides. I called the gas company and had them suspend service for three months, called the post office and had my mail held. He sat on my sofa, observing these preparations, and I told him about my sketchy itinerary: ten days, time for stops at the Grand Canyon, Joshua Tree, maybe the California coast. I'd made many long car trips alone and knew I didn't like to rush.

Then I thought, why not? *Do you want to go with me?* I asked, nervous, excited. It was a lark; we had shared a few dinners, flirted, but despite my infatuation, I knew we were nothing to each other. Still I held my breath and waited.

He took out an emergency loan for gas money. We left Houston on a Tuesday.

▨ ▨ ▨

We started out fast and picked up speed along the way. Outside our sleek windows, Houston's coastal plain turned into the limestone scarp and gray-green scrub of the Hill Country, then west Texas' scoured hills, studded with prickly pear. The shoulder of I-10 glittered with broken glass, and silver trucks barreled beside us in the left lane. We burned into El Paso and pulled over, not to rest but to refuel, and while the gas gulped through the black hose and into the tank, we ran around and around the car, savoring the feel of moving our legs after so long, making the blood pump, waving our arms and shouting, a mile short of New Mexico.

The days ran together. We slept, when we slept, in run-down motels, or forest land, or in the car. Once, near Sedona, on the ground a few yards from the road; once, in the Kaibab, on a cleared hillock by a pile of ragged pines. Green light in the warm morning tent. Red buttes cluttered with boulders. Folded bills left under a chipped dinner plate. The tiled floors of dozens of public restrooms. Dancing in a cramped barroom, drinking from his salted mouth. A bleary-eyed watchman in Las Cruces, the motel lobby smelling of asafoetida and curry. Most nights we didn't sleep, most mornings stayed in bed past checkout (housekeepers hammering on thin doors, hollering for us to leave). The back seat accumulated flotsam: coin-op trinkets; maps of Arizona, California, Colorado, Utah; postcards from gas stations, with pictures of gas stations on them; a piñon cone, and a bristlecone, cast off from the world's oldest living thing; empty soda cans. Roll after roll of film, but these don't tell the story. Some days I think I've forgotten, then memory broadsides me: I'm back in a strip-mall Chinese restaurant, Reno, knowing we have one last night together, and the bottom drops out. How would I relearn solitude?

Four snapshots: One. Leaving the room key on the nightstand, next to last night's empty bottle of red, we walk across the street to a diner where even the windows are greasy and order something called The Pile, grill-cleaner's special, square-cut potatoes and jalapeño slices wilted from the heat, chunks of chorizo and fried egg spattered with melting strings of jack cheese. Coffee oily and hot. By the time we leave it's past noon and we're westbound on I-10, slicing the bottom off New Mexico. Sun bright as a magnesium flare.

Two. He shaves before a beveled mirror. There's a spot on his neck he can't reach. *Could you help me?* he asks. Even as I dip the razor in suds and draw it over the rough place, I think, *This is what a wife would do.*

Three. Black midnight in a place with no towns, and topping a rise to see the electric glitter of Las Vegas stretched from horizon to horizon, bright and blinking, demarcating sand from sky, straight as a plucked chalk line and burning all night and day, a star this close to bursting.

Four, the last. Inside a whitewashed chapel, adobe walls covered with paintings of round-faced children, a couple prepare to renew their vows. The alcove behind them overflows with pillar candles, cut daisies in water-filled jam jars, cloth dolls, wax-spattered photos. The rough-hewn benches are painted turquoise. There are no guests but us, two strangers, and as the couple and their priest make ready, they smile at each other and at us. We will slip out the back. But not before he pulls me near, quiet, asks me to marry him. At first I think he is joking, but his eyes are serious and I say *yes,* I say, *someday.*

▪ ▪ ▪

We drove through the last night to make his flight in Seattle. The airport doors slid shut behind him. I put the car in gear and drove off, slowly, alone, through the Yakima Valley, where cherry and apple orchards marched past the empty passenger seat. Crossing the Columbia at The Dalles, I wound south into Oregon, the sun setting behind distant Mount Hood, and driving felt like drowning, swelling up and down over land shaped by the ancient roll of shallow seas, by tides of basalt flowing from blood-red volcanoes. Even though the summer sun sets late there, full dark found me still driving, and it was nearly midnight before I unlocked the little trailer by park headquarters that would be my home for the next three months. I fell asleep in the sleeping bag that still smelled of us. So the summer began.

My days shaped themselves into a pattern. Dawn broke early, sun pouring in the trailer windows at four, and I rose. Most mornings I had kayak floats, so I drove the truck to the boat ramp and unloaded the boats on the beach. When the campers arrived, we put in our kayaks where oil rainbows filmed the water and paddled upstream, under the suspension bridge and past the houseboats, where the canyon walls were too narrow for bigger boats to go. Upstream, things were quiet, no wake to ride, no fumes. In the shallow, clear water you could see boulders long tumbled from the scree piles on the banks. Water mosses like tiny trees grew on them, waving when we J-stroked over, and the water glittered with mica. When we got too tired to paddle, I told the campers about the geology of the place, the mulleins that flung up columns on the banks, bald eagles, the hydroelectric dam. Fish flashed between the rocks, and orioles hung their sock nests in the alder thickets.

Once, we saw an osprey circling high overhead, above the canyon rim. When it spotted a leaping kokanee it dove, plummeting three hundred feet to the surface of the lake, plunging its feet into the water, and rose, the fat fish wriggling in its talons. Then it circled just over our heads, as if showing us its prize, and made for its nest, where I knew it would rip the fish's guts out and feast, dripping. But I liked the common birds best: magpies, western jays, cliff swallows in their violet tailcoats. They darted and dropped, swooping, catching insects in their sieve-like beaks; their flight looked tipsy.

On one of the kayak floats, a Wednesday, we met the crawfisherman. Friendly, sunburned, he showed us the dog kibble he used for bait; we watched him dump his take, arching and flailing, into plastic buckets. He pointed out the ledge where he'd seen a mountain lion hunched over a mule deer. *Looked up when he saw me,* he said, *but didn't stop what he was doing.* Not many mornings after that, someone spotted the crawfisherman's boat drifting slowly across the lake; nearby, a pale form bobbed in the water: the crawfisherman himself, naked as the day he was born. The first desert drowning of the season.

The coroner figured it out: the crawfisherman's boat must have tugged loose from the dock, and he'd stripped to the skin and jumped in after it. His heart pulled him up short before he could catch the tether. I don't know who found him, but I remember the first I heard about it: his shirt, pants, socks, and shoes were stacked neatly on the dock, but no one ever found his underwear. *Guess he liked to go commando,* a ranger kidded, and I hated her for joking about it. The empty margarine tubs of kibble he used to attract the crawfish: it takes an effort to remember these. But I can't escape the absence of his underwear.

After that, I always thought of the crawfisherman when we passed the ledge where he'd seen the cougar, high on the canyon wall, near the cut where the exposed rock showed the strata of long years: volcanic rubble and above it fine gray ash, smooth river cobbles, a layer of iron-rich red, iron-poor charcoal, and above that thin topsoil and prairie bunchgrass. Above that stunted sage. Above that sky.

Afternoons were my slow time. When I arrived, the park manager told me that hikes, crafts, and history talks—mainstays of most interpretive programs—would not be well attended at the Cove. The lake is the draw, even in a typical year, and 2001 was atypical. A hard drought hit Oregon that year, and other reservoir lakes were tapped for irrigation; by midsummer, they were nothing but stumps and cracked mud, and Lake Billy was the only lake in the state at full pond. So in the afternoon, I did a lot of waiting around, planning programs nobody showed for because they were off playing in the water. To pass the time, I hiked the Tam-a-Lau ("Land of Standing Boulders," in Wasco) trail from the campground to the plateau.

Near the trailhead, leathery lichen clung to a rock. When I poured my canteen over it, the lichen swelled and sent up spore-tipped filaments before my eyes, so ready was it for rain. Further up the trail lay the chalk-marked boulders where climbers illegally practiced. Although they probably didn't notice, there was an old ochre painting on a nearby rock. The reddish smears could have been an animal or a crouching human figure; I couldn't tell. One of the rangers planted seedlings next to the rock, in an effort to hide the drawing from possible vandals, but the soil was too dry and the trees kept dying. *Give this one a drink whenever you can,* he told me once. *It needs all the help we can spare.*

Even the plants had histories; to hike past was to read characters written in leaf and stalk. Tall spikes of wooly mullein, hagweed, grew on the canyon slopes; ancient Greeks, I had read, dipped the stalks in tallow for funeral torches. In the disturbed soil along the trail's edge, cheatgrass thrived, choking the native bluestem and medusa-head grasses. Cheatgrass deserves its bitter name. The homesteaders who tried to settle eastern Oregon bought wheat and rye back home, hauling the seed across the country with them. They sowed it carefully, but when it sprouted they found that the good seed had been larded with weed, and it was much too late to demand the seller make it right. Now the homesteaders are gone, but the cheatgrass still sprouts every year, circling the old juniper trees, surviving where nothing else can.

When I think of central Oregon, I think first of juniper and sage, two plants that dominated that landscape, wrenching shade from dry soil and sun. The juniper at noon smelled of sweat and pine; at dusk its laddered profile painted the sand in black strokes. I loved the tenacious juniper from root to gum-stippled needle, particularly a gnarled individual three centuries old on the canyon rim, a tree that despite its age stood only ten feet tall, a tree rived from repeated lightning strikes, whose skinny stitch of bark and needle pulled life from rock. The juniper survived, adding another layer of wood every season. This one, because it carried no berries, dendrologists would call a "bachelor"; covered in pollen, it scattered its dry yellow decade after decade. Of the juniper, John Muir said, "It dies

standing, and wastes insensibly out of existence like granite."
Settlers, both Wasco and white, had tried and failed to live on
that plateau, but the juniper remains, with its companion sagebrush, silver leaves lobed like jackrabbit tracks, fine-furred and
dark-veined. After rain, sage gave off a sharp tang, vegetal and
sweet. Bushes without number stretched to the horizon, like
green lambs crouching, pale heads tucked between their knees.

But my favorite part of the trail was an old homestead site
on the canyon rim. Beside a cleared rectangle where a cabin
had been there stood a lava wall, built when the homesteaders cleared their fields for planting. About fifty yards long and
wider than my arms could reach, the lava wall was made of
red, burnt-looking rocks, air pocked and light enough to toss.
Bits of old refuse lay scattered about: tin cans flaked with rust,
shards of glass turned purple from decades of sun, fragments
of a china plate painted with rosebuds. Orange barbed wire
sprouted from the ground like a wind-blasted weed. A pair of
fence lizards flashed their brilliant blue underbellies at me when
I ventured too close. Everything was of a piece with the dusty
desert; the broken glass and rusted tin seemed to have been
exuded by the place just as much as the chunks of stippled lava
and the clutches of bunchgrass. The homesteaders, gone now,
had risked their lives to get here, and in the span of a lifetime,
the place they couldn't wrestle a living from had been overrun
with petulant children from the city across the mountain pass.
All these visitors left was their trash. I was surprised to love it
most of all I found that summer.

Standing on the edge of the plateau, I'd look down into the
canyon campground, where red and purple dome tents sat in
the shade of cottonwood trees. Compared to the dull green
of the juniper, the cottonwood was a flashy tree, its leaves acid
green backed with whitewash, shaking in the wind with a
sound like rain. Coddled in their protected canyon spot, their
roots laved with bathhouse runoff, cottonwoods led a pam-
pered existence, and I just couldn't respect them as I did the

junipers. But the cottonwoods were hospitable; in their spreading branches porcupines lived, drowsing in the long afternoons, gnawing bark at night, and sloughing occasional needles, which I hunted: beautiful splinters, hollow as blowpipes.

During that summer, a revolving throng of campers made the grounds their home, swelling its population to nearly that of Madras, the county seat. The campers crowded through the gate, jamming the road with fifth-wheels and pop-ups, boats on trailers, and motor homes the size of charter buses. The campers sat inside, silent behind smoked-glass windows, air conditioners dripping condensation on the dark asphalt. They were waiting to check in, to sign the forms and get the Xeroxed map of the campground so they could back carefully into their reserved spots, set the parking brake, and stretch their legs. Or stretch their tarps; I witnessed frustrated parents mutter and curse as they tried to set up tents, still dusty from last year, without benefit of instructions. The motor-home crowd pulled out their green canvas awnings, unrolled strips of all-weather carpet, unfolded lawn chairs, and staked carved-wood signs showing their names and hometowns by their site numbers. They leashed their little dogs and took them for an airing, carrying Ziploc baggies for the waste; they bought bundles of firewood for their iron fire pits. At night, generators hummed, porcupines stirred sleepily in the treetops, and the night ranger made slow rounds in his green golf cart, its electric motor purring. The campground smelled of wood smoke and burned sugar, sunscreen and roasting meat, diesel.

During preparations for an especially busy weekend, the park manager explained part of my job description that he hadn't mentioned before; I was to know one J. R. Beaver very well. Our conversation went something like this:

We were thinking, with Memorial Day coming up, J. R. Beaver might make an appearance. (Get the suit out of the closet, will you?) *Maybe I forgot to tell you about it over the phone. J. R. Beaver, you know, he's the mascot for the Oregon Parks and Rec. Makes*

rounds of the campgrounds every Friday and Saturday afternoon,
when most families arrive. Here's the background information (sheaf
of paper). *Most important thing, make sure and wear the ice packs,*
last year we had somebody pass out, one of the hotter days. In that
suit, it's always going to be a hot day, right? Ha ha. Wear the ice,
we don't want you getting sick. Second most important thing: J.R.
doesn't talk. Give the kids high five; they like that. But no talking, it
scares them. Don't forget your head (large circular hatbox). *Reshape*
the hat, it always gets smashed in the off season. Knock 'em dead!

So began the most surreal episode of my time as a park
ranger.

Before everything, the vest with ice pockets. Then the foam
barrel, zip-front suit, broad tail-paddle. Great feet, held on with
nylon-strap sandals. And last of all, the beach-ball-sized head
with Styrofoam teeth and mesh eyespots from which I peered.
I got stuck in doors and golf-cart seats because of my wide
rump. I tottered around the campground, frightening children
and giving randy uncles a chance to make yet another stupid
beaver joke.

In my info packet, I'd read about J.R.'s Secret Greeting; in
the campground, I discovered, it was so secret that no one rec-
ognized it. A cousin of the "Aloha—hang loose" sign, you make
it by pointing your index and pinky fingers, then bending the
middle and ring fingers and rubbing them against each other in
a supposed imitation of beaver teeth. Wild beavers have bright
orange teeth that never stop growing. If the animal did not con-
stantly wear down its teeth by chewing on tough tree branches,
the teeth would grow longer and longer, curving down to pierce
its lower jaw and causing death by starvation. J.R. managed to
avoid this problem.

Kids' responses to J.R. varied. Some were fascinated—"Nice
beavuh," lisped one blond tot—but most were terrified, and fled
if they could. "Hey, there's a *person* in there," said the more perceptive of the older kids. "Are you hot? Huh? Huh? Are you
hot in there?" And then there were the inevitable confusions

among those less schooled in mammal identification. "Hey, it's Smokey Bear!" I pointed irritably to my considerable tail. "He's a *beaver*," my wrangler would point out, patiently.

Some evenings, I led campers on short night hikes designed to raise their sensory awareness. Can you identify these smells: coffee, soap, juniper, sagebrush? If you listen for sixty seconds, what will you hear? One night we heard a thin scream, definitely not human, coming from the near distance. "Golden eagle?" one of the hikers asked, hopefully. "Naw, it's a Nerf football," a kid said, and it turned out he was right.

On nights when I didn't have programs, I'd sit in the shade of my trailer reading in a tilted chair, watching the light fade from Lake Billy. From the lake came the occasional purr of a motorboat, but mostly things were quiet. The lake teemed with kokanee salmon that leaped from the water, flashing in the sun; their flesh tasted of bright July and butter. The little radio I'd brought pulled in a lone station, staticky country, and I kept it on for company. Mice stumbled drunkenly along the baseboards and collapsed where they fell, too dazed to go for the peanut-butter-baited traps I set out. Rattlesnakes dozed in the cool dust under the laundry shed.

On Wednesday and Saturday evenings at eight, he'd call me on the campground pay phone. He read Rilke while I watched campers start smoky fires and the camp host lowered the flag; he put the phone next to his guitar and sang me songs. I told him about the porcupines shambling past the Coke machine, and he told me about the terrible flood that wiped out twenty years of cancer research at the hospital downtown. We talked as the light faded, stars came out, and coyotes screamed; we talked so much that the phone company disconnected him and he had to call from a gas-station pay phone on Studemont Boulevard.

After hanging up, I'd walk, invisible, up the warm asphalt road to my trailer, or down to the old boat dock that rocked gently in the water. I lay on my back, watching a hail of meteors. One night a boat drifted by, motor cut, people on deck laughing boozily. *Is somebody there?* I heard them say. *What if there's somebody there?*

It was a place unlike any I had known, and I tried to understand it, to figure it out somehow: anything to distract myself from how alone I felt. I thought the place deserved a better creation story than the one it had: *crushing all opposition, Big Electric throttles three rivers.* Say instead *the reservoir's green water dropped like slag from a glass factory;* say *green water filled this hurt, rose like sap in a deep-rooted tree.* Say *a strong woman cut a line in the ground, fitted a wedge to that groove, swung a mallet made from pine bole and chert head, swung it and cracked the earth like an egg made of stone.* Like thunder eggs, Oregon's state rock, lumpy rounds showing earth and sky inside when diamond wheels bite them open. Polished smooth and purple like the canyon rim at sunset.

It had taken millions of years for the land to shape itself into what I saw, ages of buckling and slow erosion, creeping lava flows, water slicing a canyon for itself, wind rasping boulders to pebbles, sand, powder. Ninety years since the homesteaders yanked sage from their fields and read about methods of dry farming. Forty years since the Christmas floods created Lake Billy. I was there for only three months, the blink of an eye, yet time behaved strangely; I couldn't get used to it. It was a long, slow season, where sunlight lingered eighteen hours, and in the brief, cool nights, I was not tired. (In July, when the mint leaves ripen, the fields at midnight release a sweet green smell. At dawn the irrigation systems begin again: *chick, chick, chick.*) I had time on my hands: to finish *A Light in August,* to start *The Remembrance of Things Past,* to write stacks of postcards and check the mailbox. Time to learn the names of the native bunchgrasses, to hike up to the canyon rim, where cougar prints marked the sand, to lead kayak floats that started in the cool morning, stepping into cold and rank-smelling water, and ended when the sun was high overhead and sweat ran down my arms. Time to talk; he always called when he promised he would. All of this, and the day not yet done. Time to boil water for pasta, under the fluorescent light in the kitchenette. Time to lay down to sleep, listening to the cottonwood's rattle, to the coyotes whose cries woke me not long after. Geologic ages; a scant century; a single summer. This season marked their intersection—three rivers met, and at their confluence, a lake rose and stretched itself out. Thousands came to see it, for reasons of their own, none of us suspecting what the others were about.

▩ ▩ ▩

Days off, I traveled, camping alone in dripping redwood forests and by the rushing banks of the Rogue and the McKenzie, hunting blue periwinkle shells at Crescent City, and whale watching on a charter boat in Depoe Bay, violently seasick. I saw where long-ago lava flows immolated trees, leaving nothing but the impress of bark; I saw tidal pools with sea stars the color of grape Kool-Aid; I saw how Tillamook cheddar was made. I hiked five thousand vertical feet to the top of South Sister, once called Charity, on the last day of July; fresh snow dusted the mountain's summit. I breathed the thin air of 10,342 feet and looked down on Mount Bachelor, jade-colored glaciers, a bright cirque lake, and, far below, the tree line. Rock cairns marked the way. I hiked a high mountain up and down that day, picking my way in the dark through the bottomland trees, and when I finally reached my car my legs were so useless I had to lift them up and place them in the seat. Other mountains are higher; even in Oregon, Mount Hood and Mount Jefferson outrank South Sister. But I climbed that summit, and I did it alone.

It's only now, years later, that I see something of what I hungered for then. Instinct pulled me to the desert and I went without knowing why, just as shortening days impel the bear to eat more: fat for the coming winter, solitude for the coming togetherness. I walked the desert with my head down, looking for interesting things, my mind elsewhere. Still my season there fed some hunger I didn't know I had; in that strange flow of time when distractions were few, I found I could get along alone. Many have gone to the desert seeking what I found, the hard blessing of solitude.

Now with him I dance an old dance, together and apart. What joy I find in talking with him. I know that conversation is a gift, because I have done without, could do without again if I had to—but how I would feel the lack.

Try, just for a moment, to believe as the homesteaders did. If the rain follows the plow, maybe then he came to me from my need, my hunger pulling him, though neither of us knew it. Maybe it's true. Today we watched doves drop like rain from a black maple; yesterday I felt his throated speech thrum beneath my fingertips; this morning I woke with him, convinced we had just dreamed the same dream. All these things are mine, but I've given something up, too: late at night, by the lake, meteors pitch toward earth, and I'm not there to see it. A solitary life I turned away from. A life another woman lived.

▪ ▪ ▪

We know little about her, save that she took a homestead under her name, alone. Histories of the place help to fill the gaps, but her particular story is lost. I found myself thinking about her, wondering why she had moved to the same place I had, what her days had been like; it was easy for me to imagine a loneliness for her, because I had ached so when I lived there. I liked to think she left home, wherever it was, with a mate, that they made the long trip—what took us days would have taken them months— together, as long as they could, that when he took sick she stayed with him, hoping, until the end. When the time came to sign for the land claim, she signed alone.

Maybe sometimes, just before sleep, fragments of the journey came back to her. She remembered mule deer in the evening's first dark, bright eyes reflecting firelight, noses snuffing a strange smell on the air. The deer's sharp panting startled her. Then they scattered, the quick thump of their hooves fading. In the morning the dewy grass trampled and broken. Maybe moments like this came upon her without warning, and she caught herself believing that when the time of harvest came, he would return.

It took years of living on the land to earn the deed, and the seasons passed slowly. In July, the copper sun shivered behind dust clouds as she worked the rows; in January, snow drifted in sculpted waves around the junipers, and the river glazed with ice. Wood smoke rafted from the lava-stone chimney she'd built, erased the risen stars. By April, orioles were knitting nests of gathered grasses, and she could taste the thaw in the air. She poured out her life like water, and this was her reward: in 1914, the government awarded her, Lora Smith Miller, the title to 160 acres. Now her name is all that's left.

No letters or gravestone, no diary: her legacy would seem invisible, but the bare fact of her existence moved me. That summer, I apprenticed myself to her, hardly knowing I was doing so. *Here is how to live a day alone; here is how to pass the night in a narrow bed. Here is how to face a question without distraction.* I made a poor student, but I stuck it out. What did I do with the time on my hands? I wished myself among friends; I found I would not make a hermit. This is something worth knowing.

Maybe waking from a dream of loss, she looked over her acres, blinding in the morning sun, and thought, *This is my portion, for a little while.* (Painting on the trailside boulder.) How long will I stay? Time spreads out, sometimes, like a braided river, or turns solid as hard-frozen ice. (Rusted tin cans and snarls of barbed wire.) A day can feel like an eternity, founded on something frail as a line of bright green shoots, the beginning of her rye field, a sight that thrilled and frightened her: the hope the leaves begot. (Children chasing each other around a dome tent; a campfire flinging sparks and smoke into the night air.) A constellation of events brought me to this place. What will I do with this hour?

Then I think she wrapped a scarf around her head and walked outside to the shed, returned with an armful of wood; fed the cookstove fire, shut the clanging damper to keep the heat. The weather was starting to turn. About the same time as last year, about what she'd had reason to expect.

Two Weddings
(Venice; South Carolina)

Venice is a city stuffed full: flowering plaster and crumble, blank postcards and dry pens, women talking and tatting falls of lace, knotted bead-strings hung from hooks, gold-sprayed paper masks, vegetable peels floating on oily water. Showrooms full of glass blown, spun, molded, and pulled, sparkling chandeliers heavy with baubles, and how could you possibly choose only one? Beneath an arched bridge, the produce sellers tie boats loaded with knobby mandarins, glossy bulbs of fennel, earth-crusted potatoes, stubby carrots.

On a certain auspicious afternoon, an important man—his identity changes—rows a narrow boat into the Grand Lagoon. The crowd, gathered on sidewalks and bridges, waits patiently, knowing what to expect but still interested. The man in the boat raises his arms high above his head, pauses, and, with great ceremony, drops a golden ring into the water. The crowd cheers: things have gone off just as they should. Venice and the sea are joined, wedded, and for centuries the doge has rowed to the middle of the water and done exactly this. Cynics claim he ties a thread to the ring, and after dropping it into the water for the benefit of those assembled, he fishes it back and saves it for next year. Who can say whether these things are true? The ceremony continues even today.

Venice on a cloudy day is a lover certain of being spurned, just shy of sullen, gnawing her wrist and staring dully out the window. But inside a fire burns behind the grate. The mosaic floors of San Marco buckle and swim; every year the heavy church sinks a little on its ancient pilings. Brass bands play out-of-tune marches in the middle of footrace routes, and lean runners with numbers pinned to their chests dodge between the slouching musicians. At midday, people wander into cafés, eat polenta dark with salty squid ink, drink tumblers of black wine. Above them mourning doves bank and sweep, stroking swift through the sky. And these daily things make a marriage: not what I expected—few grand gestures—but sometimes the savory smell of sage and butter reducing, sometimes stewed tomatoes, sometimes soap and a clean-swept floor.

Months pass. The sea laps gently at the canal walls, rises, filling the cobbled streets. Townspeople walk to market on temporary pathways made of banquet tables. Their soles drip; at home, pairs of stockings decorate radiators, drying. Slowly the city sinks, and the water swirls higher, covering the dark mold marks on the piers, flooding the low-lying shops, until the earth tilts away from the moon and the water drains through sluices covered with iron grates. And on the appointed day, a man again weds the water. The lagoon bottom piled with old love-tokens. The water above them unmarked as ever.

▨ ▨ ▨

Say I wedded the place I love, late at night and alone, one pledge, one ceremony not to be repeated. Say I cut the clay with a sharp spade and planted there a slip of weed; say I buried my shoes, the soles slick from much walking, split past repair. Mark a line on my body and let the blood run down, for marriage calls for something more than a gold ring; marriage calls for the blood of a woman. The question is not, *How much will it take?* but *How much will you give?* Say I turned the spade and the earth was red already. Not the first lover, not the last. And so every day I pay my due, calling things by their rightful names, taking into my body the elements (water, light) of life, every day falling more deeply into debt.

Chihuahua Desert Love Song

DAWN

Down by the river stands the little brown burro on haunches narrow and trembling as a girl's.

MORNING

Although the river here is shallow enough to wade, men launch their dented aluminum boats into the current, poling across with long staves. For two dollars apiece they ferry travelers over and back, peeling change from a roll of sweat-damp bills. We travelers stay dry, the men make a living; this is a good arrangement.

MIDDAY

By noon the sun's an anvil pressing down on my nape and the bleached wall of the Sierra del Carmen stands out sharp as a theater backdrop. Creosote's oily yellow leaves radiate their sharp smell, and the Boke button's single flower bares its bright throat. Horse dung drying on the trail is grass and the earth where grass grows. Nothing is wasted, nothing unclean. The desert is silent as a sheet of paper; when you blink, I hear it, eyelids' fluttering kiss.

AFTERNOON

Across the road from a dead century plant, twenty-foot bloom stalk bent on the ground, yellow leaves splayed like a dropped hand of cards, a silversmith sits in the striped shade of an ocotillo-cane ramada, wares spread on a draped table. Though I have no money, he hands me a ring set with polished agate. "Mail me a check when you get home," he says. "There's not enough trust in the world." Surprised, vaguely flattered, I slide the ring on my finger; tilting the stone, I can just make out the marks of the polisher's wheel.

Sundown

When the wind kicks up, the pads of dead prickly pear clatter like bones. Dark falling fast and hard, we walk to camp, passing beneath the single telephone line. Invisible, crackling, the telephone wire hums with talk, carrying conversation to the end of the line, where the river marks the border. Above us, the stars slide coldly toward dawn. That night I dream of needles pulled, red, from calf and palm, and wake aching on cold ground.

Morning

Leaving, we find a bleached coyote skull, teeth brown from its last kill. When I stumble, careless, the barbed end of a lechuguilla rives my shin, lodging close to the bone, a hard lump. I tape the salved wound closed. Twelve days. When I pull the risen splinter, the wound weeps water, unmixed with blood.

Afterward

Something says, you can make a place here, if you are careful. Others have: witness the telephone line's crackling current of talk, battered boats scraping the riverbank. Candelilla and yucca, hedgehog cactus and dog turd cholla; jackrabbit, roadrunner, Chihuahua raven; the tiny-hooved, myopic javelina, foraging near the riverbed. Also two tall cowboys in tight jeans and jingling spurs; I watch them walk into the general store,

their eyes hooded against the strong sun. The sandstone hoodoos along Panther Gap Road change a little every day, usually
in ways too small to measure—wind gnaws deeper in a curve, or
grates a few grains of rock from the ridge—but once, a ranger
tells me, a pillar there one evening was gone next morning, a
heap of boulders where it had stood. Wind working in a rotten
seam. That dust has drifted, now, into the pleated yucca, settled
in the part of someone's hair, swirled downstream where I can't
go. Desert mosaic of many-colored pebbles. Ribbed barrel cactus swelling and shrinking in rain and drought. Look at all I've
smuggled out, splinter rooted under skin, silver band circling
my finger, silence hid beneath my tongue.

Dust Devils

At noon, the silent desert demands metaphor. I have watched the burned land shiver, have felt my own eyes sting. The desert then is like a geode, and the sun's a hammer cracking it; split, shattered, the dull sphere shows itself to be lined with quartz. Light glints from beveled planes. Those crystals formed, so slowly, in darkness thick enough to be felt. Darkness that evaporates on touching the hot desert air, or drains into a tin can's shadow. The desert at midday is the hidden made known; the desert at midday (might) explain things. The sun's a jackboot on my sweaty nape.

Here lives the magpie, handsome and intelligent bird, neatly turned out in dark tailcoat and white shirtwaist, sateen swelling over a full breast, every seam nipped to fit. Like the crows and jays, his sociable kin, he seeks bright things and steals them when he can. I've seen his swooping flight, when with folded wings he drops to the ground, pierces a garbage bag with a jab, and plucks his prize. A man once told me that a young magpie may be taught to speak if a patient master notches its tongue. But I hate this precise violence, this forced entry to voice. *Chuck chuck* cries the still-whole magpie, his language not ours. What else would he have to say?

An old story. The elder of two princesses marries and moves to a far country. Months pass, and she grows lonely for her sister, so her husband goes to fetch her for a visit. But the wargod's cruel blood runs in the husband's veins and, smitten by his sister-in-law's beauty, he rapes her and cuts out her tongue when she swears to tell. Deprived of speech, unable to write—for writing doesn't yet exist—she weaves his treachery into a vivid tapestry and sends it to her sister who, overwhelmed by her husband's crime, despairs of a way to show him her hatred.

Just then her only child runs into the room.

No boy ever looked more like his father.

She slices his throat and drains his blood into a kettle of stew hanging over the fire. Spoon clinks against bowl; sodden linen in the lap. A quiet meal.

When her husband, sated, pushes away from the table, she tells him what he's eaten, then flies with her silent sister to the wilderness. He's swift with rage, and his sword's edge flashes in the trembling sun; just as the blade grazes the nearer sister's nape, the gods transform the women into birds. Voiceless Philomena becomes the twittering sparrow, and Procne, the nightingale, forever dirges the son she murdered.

Another story. When the Pharisees bring a woman caught in adultery to Christ and demand that he condemn her, he ignores them and bends to write with his finger in the dust. This is the only instance of his writing that the Gospels record. *Let he who is without sin cast the first stone,* he says, and continues to write until they leave. Only then does he raise his head and look at the woman, left standing alone before him. *Go and sin no more,* he says, thus restoring her to life and its blessed quotidian babble.

Dust devils spindle across the desert, tight funnels of whirling sand. From this distance, they are silent, moving erratically across the flatlands, vanishing. From here to the horizon is no house, tree, sign, or body. Only cars, mute and glassy, their windows flashing as they pass, silver freightliners, and dust devils, dervishes tracing letters in the sand, writing what no one can read, erasing as they go.

II.

Beyond the Wilderness

I stood in a clearing, she said, much later. *Light all around, but darkness above me. Looked up and saw something falling from the sky, fast, something heavy, something dark. Too fast for me to stop.* She knew it would strike. *I put my arm up to cover my head,* a reflex; it would do no good. *Oh God, I said.* And then it hit.

I.

As gunmetal clouds piled in the west, he ate his simple meal (sandwich, apple) and sheltered in the mouse-smelling dark of the hunters' shack. Rain came hard, battering the standing corn, streaking the leaves with soupy dirt. Lightning forked over the woods, and he saw it out of the corner of his eye as he stared at that storied ground, thinking about something or other. Near the north boundary line was a spot where people said an Indian princess had been buried, and in the back field, a symmetrical hill sloped up to a shelf, then down again. People said it was a mound made for some kind of harvest ritual. He didn't know one way or the other, but plowed it every spring and watered the shoots that grew there.

2.

In Logan County, central Ohio, the seasons are distinct, enthusiastic. Spring (black-turned earth) can break your heart with hope, summer (golden corn in the silo) is hotter than you think possible, winter (dark trees, curling smoke) lasts forever.

But this is an autumn story, and just as the other seasons have their colors, so does autumn—brown, for potatoes, for shadows in the empty barn, for frost-killed stalks lying broken on cold ground, for months that leave nothing behind but the land's very shape. Hills curved like a well-loved body. Pond water like chrome, then sunset, and light drains from everything.

My father's father was a hired man on a farm in Logan County. One of eleven children, he'd been raised poor, wrapping himself in newspapers to get through the bitter winters. He worked hard his whole life, just to get by, doing whatever job he could find. Many a farmhouse around there had a roof he'd nailed or siding he'd painted, and he'd swept the schoolhouse floors, driven the bus. But Prall's farm was the work of his life. Ever since he turned fourteen, he'd been plowing and seeding Prall's fields, cutting and stacking and pitching his hay, spreading his cows' manure. My grandfather tended another man's land until the day he died and later, when they thought of it, his sons would say, *That's just the way things were then.*

His wife, my father's mother, worked for decades in the hospital's laundry, a job that suited her firecracker energy. She never missed a shift. Years of scrubbing her neighbors' stubborn blood from sheets taught her every trick for getting rid of the stains a hurting body makes. This was just the work she did for pay; at home she worked harder still. The little four-room house, built long before by runaway slaves, had a floor that canted on its foundation and a bucket of well water that froze hard on winter nights. She stuffed newsprint into the gaps in the wall and papered over so it wouldn't show, raised four boys on potatoes and little else, took baths in the cellar once a week, used a three-seat outhouse out back. She scoured the kitchen floor on her hands and knees, even at the end; she said it cleaned better than a mop.

When winter broke and sap rose in the maple trees, he collected metal spouts from the cans where he kept them, bored holes in the trunks, and hung buckets from nails. He poured full buckets into the sugar shed's great keeping tank and fed the fire all through the night, resting sometimes, smelling dust and old birds' nests, the sweet fog of bubbling sugar. When the sap shrank after long boiling, he pulled it off into cans with *Prall's Syrup* painted on the side. If this touched his pride, it was one of many things he never mentioned.

Once the snow melted, he kept an eye out for mushrooms. The calendar was no help; it had to do with a feeling in the air, a certain cool dampness, with a warm breeze promising that the lilacs and peonies of Memorial Day and beyond would bud and bloom again this year. He could taste when it was time, and as he went about his work, he looked for the pointed tops of morels pushing through the leaf litter; he stepped off the trail and through the maypops, lifting the leaves with the side of his hand. In a good year he filled bag after bag with mushrooms plucked from rotten logs, from the shadow of spreading walnut or hickory. He soaked them in salt water overnight and fried them next day in flour and fat; they tasted of nuts and molasses, yeasty—like earth, like dough.

She dreamed, sometimes, of things to come. She knew the pregnancies of other women before they knew themselves, thickening bud of red-tulip flesh: she knew. Of the teenaged granddaughter and, too, the anxious daughter-in-law. To her she said, *Six months from now, a girl, don't worry, I had a dream about it.* (Mine was that predicted birth.) She dreamed of change but kept it to herself, biding her time.

So passed fifty seedtimes and harvests, most marked by some event: the year he laid irrigation pipe in the back field; the year she bore their last son; the year of the great potato harvest. Their four sons grew to men, married, had children of their own. The span of a life cannot be summed up in a few lines. But this is all I have—nothing written in their hands—this, and what I've seen myself. Arms and napes creased from years of sun; hands knuckled and knobbed from long working.

Fall came hard in 1980, real snow by Election Day, dead berry canes rattling in a cold wind. In the slow time that followed, he caught up on chores he'd let slide during the busy harvest season. He tied new insulation around the cellar pipes, honed and oiled summer tools and wrapped them in rags, noticed the woodpile wasn't as substantial as it ought to have been. So he took his chain saw into the woods to clear some brush. It was a gray Wednesday in late November, Thanksgiving eve, and he planned to get home early.

It was a path he'd walked countless times. He scanned the trees on either side of the tractor trail, looking for dead wood, and when he saw a snag he turned aside, pulled the cord, and heard the chain saw rip to life. Safely upslope, clear of the fall line, he touched the saw to the trunk and sawdust streamed down.

The work he did required a great deal of selective awareness. He was practically deaf, for instance, to the chain saw, but alert to the crack of a falling branch. The vibrating saw masked the tree's smaller movements, but within the thrumming undercurrent he felt the tree shift as it gave. He knew there were risks, had had his share of close calls, but trusted himself implicitly; he had to. Then he heard the rotten crunch of a limb, looked up, and breathed *Oh God*. Just as she had dreamed he would.

3.

> (Moses) led his flock beyond the wilderness, and came to Horeb, the mountain of God.... "I must turn aside and look at this great sight, and see why the bush is not burned up."... (He) hid his face, for he was afraid to look at God.
>
> EXODUS 3:1–6

Ravens croaked, flapping toward a stream bright as mica. The far slopes changed color as a cloud passed over. Flat white flowers bloomed beside him as he trudged along, lost in thought. The dusty hem of his robe swept the trailside flowers, shaking them on their stems, and he could have been blind for all he noticed. He was thinking about something—who knew what?—as his feet carried him along the familiar route. Maybe he calculated the extra forage his ewes would need for lambing; maybe he wondered whether his wife had finished the evening meal.

Then, without realizing why, he looked up, and it was like waking from a dream. When he turned his head to the right, he felt as if he'd stepped into a furnace—blasted, his eyes watering, face flaming. He saw the bush a few steps away; the air above it rippled, a braided river of flame. When a twig cracked in the heat, he jumped; that sound must have been what woke him before.

But something wasn't right. That blaze was burning hotter than most fires did, he knew, and yet the flames didn't consume the bush; its small leaves, instead of curling into ash and dropping to the ground, remained distinct, as did the limbs supporting them. He stepped off the path to investigate.

An old man, he was a herder of flocks and nothing more. That is, until he left the trail, intent on discovering the secret. He lifted a foot and placed it carefully on the desert sand, by that motion transformed from shepherd to patriarch. And approaching the fire he realized this was more than an oddity; it was a sign that—perhaps because he noticed—was meant for him. Without taking his eyes from the blaze, he reached down and unlaced first one dusty sandal and then the other, dropping them in the sand, hardly conscious of what he was doing. Standing on ground he knew was holy, he waited for the word to come.

4.

She made a casserole for the next day and cut up potatoes to fry. Outside, the afternoon faded, and she started to worry; not for the first time. She knew the dangers of working on a farm. She called her third son, my father, and asked him to go to Prall's and check.

In the gray November twilight, he parked on the side of the road and headed into the woods. Wind blew the fallen leaves in rattling clouds. His shoes crunched on the leaves and gravel; that, and the sighing wind, were the only sounds. No whining saw or chugging tractor. He didn't like it. He switched on his flashlight, sweeping its beam across the woods from right to left, over trees he had known since he was a child.

He found his father lying on the ground, one arm tucked under his body, the other, broken, flung over his head. Blood on his arm, his face; blood in dulling puddles on leaves, blood pulled away into dark soil. The blade of the chainsaw lay sunk in the groove it had dug for itself; when he picked it up, later, it wouldn't start. Ran itself out of gas.

When the coroner arrived, he said the falling branch had killed him instantly. He hadn't felt anything after the initial blow, but he had seen it coming. They knew by the way he had thrown the saw from him.

5.

I wasn't with him that cold afternoon, and yet in years since, I've watched it happen again and again. His vision struck him dumb and struck him down; there was no living witness. But a week before the accident, his wife dreamed herself in a clearing, looked up and saw something falling fast. *Oh God,* she (he) says, throwing an arm up to blunt the impact. After that, everything changed.

A few months after my grandfather's death, my father took a job in South Carolina, over five hundred miles away. I was a child, five years old, and my sister had just been born. My father had always lived in Ohio, and so had my mother, and her mother, her mother's mother. We moved south, where my sister and I grew up. Because the Bible was the book we knew best, when I think of my family's particular history, I read it in biblical terms. Like this: he had a vision, of a horror; he sent us on our way, to a place he himself would never reach. That moment of revelation, when he realized his life was about to end—he threw the saw from him—that's the moment I can't let go of. That's the moment I keep trying to read.

What about his wife, his widow? People said *it was a freak accident*; people said *he didn't suffer*; *it was the best way for him to go*. Did she wonder if she could have prevented it? If she'd said, *Maybe you could tinker around in the barn today, take it easy, tomorrow's Thanksgiving*; or, *Feels like a storm's coming*. (Wind dislodges the limb and it falls harmlessly in a hail of twigs, smashes on the leaf-drifted ground, breaks into fragments in the deserted winter woods.) Could she have convinced him? He wouldn't have listened. Bullheaded. *Got to do it*, he would have said; *you worry too much*. Cursed with the power to see her grief tearing toward her, and helpless to turn it aside.

He didn't leave much. A black-and-white photo, taken the year of the record potato harvest. He stands in the cellar of Prall's farmhouse, a potato cupped in each hand, a mountain of tubers behind him, stacked floor to rafters. In this moment, wearing his laborer's clothes and looking proud, he seems to know that sometimes hard work is rewarded, though he couldn't have known what was coming: a good death, if too soon, doing useful work in a place he loved. A life of work, siphoning sugar from trees, shucking husk and silk from corn, leavening soil with manure. I wonder what he thought about, working alone in the field day after day, making those wordless, repeated motions; he was a silent man. The wood he cut warmed another man's farmhouse through a long winter.

For a man who lived his life so tied to the seasons, it seems right that his death came for him at autumn's turning to winter. With his body he left a pair of broken glasses, a wristwatch, and a bone-handled pocketknife—vision, time, utility. To his sons

he left blunt red hands and stout fingers. He left those who
would remember him, carry his name, and I am one.

6.

The pond's ringed now with alder and cattails. Redwing black-
birds perch, crying *trunk-a-lee,* and in wet years the slate-lined
creek is full of speckled creek-chubs and shiners. Worn trails
crisscross the woods, and grass grows in the gravel he dumped
in the low places to keep the tractor from wallowing. Thickets
of brush between the oaks, sugar maples, buckeye, walnut trees;
nobody's cleared the undergrowth in years. On the neighbor-
ing farms, enormous machines with air-conditioned cabs move
slowly across the fields where, as a boy, my father hunted flint
flakes and arrowheads.

The last time my father and I visited Logan County, we
walked Prall's farm without saying much. In the old hunters' shack we sat in the dust and laddered light. While he sat
thinking I went out to the cornfield, dug a little dirt, and put it
in a plastic bag. I didn't know, then, why I did it. Now I think
the old pull toward the place was something passed on to me
unearned, like dark eyes and a tendency to hoard, fondness
for horseradish and a predilection toward eating watermelon
with a knife; there must be countless tics I carry that I think,
mistakenly, originated with me. Odd, particular, this family
inheritance.

Prall's farm hasn't been worked in years, and his grand-
children grow old. Just a matter of time, I know, until they
sell out, piecemeal, in squares and rectangles. Little houses on
cul-de-sacs for the people who work at the Honda plant down
the road. But not this. This is mine, this thing I've stolen, scant
handful of earth and root threads, taken close to the spot where
my father's father died. The dark earth took his blood, held him
close at the end. And now I'll say that land was his, never mind

whose name was inked on the deed. He signed his contract with nail-heads hammered flush, in irrigation trenches' laborious characters, in spout holes, healed now, where maple sap dripped. If I could go back to those woods, I would touch my fingers to the round scars in the bark.

The Little White House

The glass in the low window is hazy with scratches. The little dog used to get so excited when visitors walked up the lane. Propping himself against the glass, he stood on his hind legs and yelped his high-pitched yelp, body quivering, front paws raking the glass. *Fala, no need to shout,* his master might have said, wheeling slowly toward the door. But inwardly I think he was gratified by the dog's joy, and although the housekeeper tried to convince him to have the window replaced, he refused. Let happiness, usually so fleeting, for once leave its mark.

Sixty years have passed since the black Scottie dog clawed the window. Fala is long gone, but the scratches remain, as do the books laid open in the study, the mixing bowls nested inside each other in the kitchen cupboards. Everything remains as it was on that day in April 1945 when Fala's master, Franklin Delano Roosevelt, suffered a cerebral hemorrhage while sitting for a portrait. *I have a terrific pain in the back of my head,* he said, slumping. People came running and lifted him from the chair, his favorite, carried him to his narrow bed, and laid him there. A few hours later he died, another casualty of the Second World War.

I made my pilgrimage to Warm Springs on a damp January day. FDR is dear to me for his Works Progress Administration, which built Easley High's handsome red-brick auditorium, and for the Civilian Conservation Corps, which cleared the trails and raised the cabins at Table Rock. I like FDR for his Fireside Chats, which actually say something, for how he figured out what his listeners needed to hear but didn't pander. And I like him for his leadership in a war I'd argue he didn't want to fight. It's plain from the pictures how the responsibility wore on him. Remember the famous shot of FDR with

Churchill and Stalin at Yalta? How bent he looks under his black shawl, dark circles under his eyes.

I walked alone through the house, stepping carefully around the sensors that triggered canned historical interpretation. The ranger at the door told me that FDR came to Warm Springs for polio treatments, building what would come to be known as the Little White House in the winter of 1931, when he was governor of New York. This ranger pointed out that even the toilet paper in the house is original. "I celebrate its birthday in February, same time I have mine," he said. "I figure, FDR died April twelfth, and the toilet paper was probably manufactured a couple of months before that. Everything in the house is original," he said. "Everything." There it hangs, brittle as parchment, encased in Plexiglas.

That was why I'd made the trip, of course: the scratches in the door, the original toilet paper. I walked through Eleanor's room and saw my face reflected in her oval mirror. His favorite chair, the one he'd been sitting in when the stroke hit, still sags with the memory of his body. The unfinished portrait he was sitting for stands on an easel in his study. His face is colored in—mouth set in a line of mingled pride and humility, graying hair swept back from the wide forehead and dark brows. The neck of his overcoat is there, and the oxblood tie, nondescript, the kind of thing anyone might wear. But there's only a blurry sepia wash to indicate his shoulders, and where are his hands that famously held his jaunty cigarette? Not here, and maybe that doesn't matter; the eyes are most important, hollows dark. He's an old, tired man. The Yalta photos show him to look even worse. The painter has been kind.

A photo hangs in the front room of the nearby FDR museum: a man playing the accordion next to the train tracks at the Warm Springs depot. In the background, the President's crepe-swathed funeral car pulls away from the station. Tears stream down the man's face as his fingers press the keys of the accordion, its bellows half-extended.

Racks of walking canes, given to the President by individuals and groups from every state and some foreign countries, fill
a wall. Hand carved with names and dates and animals. I think
of all the time put into them. His polio was too far gone for any
of them to be of much use, but he didn't let on.

In the beginning of the Depression, my grandfather wrapped
himself in newspaper to keep warm. Years later, when I knew
him, he had odd habits: savings balled in a sock, compulsive
stockpiling of sale items. Ketchup, even. Rows of glass bottles
lined the dusty shelves of his cellar. What happened to them
after he died? They may be there still, the meager treasure. He
saved what he could.

There's a book at the Little White House where visitors old
enough to remember write where they were when they learned
of FDR's death. I paged through this. Some were vague: *Sta-
tioned at army base. Teaching.* This one was more specific: *Walking home from school. Man working in cornfield called out to me:
"Have you heard?" I ran down the dusty road. Momma sat crying
on the porch.*

My grandfather has no such book, no museum or rack of
hand-carved canes. No one ever painted his portrait. What
there is: kind black earth, rolling hills, a hay baler for sale across
the cemetery road. Beautiful, mute, he is one of millions.

Eleanor, with her formidable energy, wrote a regular newspaper column that was widely syndicated. After her husband's
death, she told the story of General Eisenhower journeying
to FDR's grave to place a wreath. When Fala heard the military cavalcade pulling up the driveway, his ears perked and he
looked around excitedly. *He must have thought his master was
coming,* Eleanor mused. *The sound of the sirens.* Remember me.
Remember me.

Bigfoot's Widow

Something about this place inspires fantasy, can make a susceptible person think of prophecies and tokens. *The wise woman of the woods bid me eat of this salad, said it would give me a vision of true love. The burbling river whispered his name to me as I slept and I woke with a certainty in my bones. If I plant the seed this tree dropped, it will grow into a strong pillar outside our well-swept door.*

So I'm not surprised that the story of Bigfoot has its genesis here, western Oregon, where the air is so thick under old-growth Douglas firs that it seems more water than gas. Where the soil is so thickly padded with fallen needles that it springs underfoot. Where the bright yellow banana slug, long as a hand, cuts its bladeless way, collecting bits of forest duff or dangling in midair from its shining self-made cord. A fantastic place requires fantastic inhabitants.

But as it turns out, Bigfoot is dead, and his widow tells us so. Bigfoot was a man, a man who held a job and paid taxes, who fathered children, who loved a practical joke. He was fortunate to have a mate who understood and even encouraged this joking. Joking takes two. She was the straight man to his punch line.

I'm betting she was the one who cut a pattern from brown paper, pinned it to the furs, sharpened a heavy pair of scissors. She sewed the seams, the needle of her machine jumping high and steady. She did nothing less than make him a new body. He read (Melville? *Time?*), sipped (brandy? decaf?), drowsed in an easy chair. Maybe he made birdhouses from scrap lumber. Maybe he planned trips to Sicily, Arizona, Bombay. Long evenings with a beloved seem endless: the oldest of lies.

In town, she bought the biggest boots she could and wrapped them with batting and leather to make them larger still. The first afternoon, she zipped him into the suit and settled the mask on his head, guided him into the truck seat, and turned the truck off the highway onto a long-abandoned logging road. Fog blurred the trees. She held the camera steady as he walked, slowly, into the woods. Did it again, working to get the best shot.

Together they developed the prints in the red-lit darkroom, laughing as the grainy images rose. It was good work; she had hidden the zipper with a thin strip of fur. It looked real. They laughed long and well, enjoying their joke. This is my hope.

And when he died, years later but much too soon, she told the truth about Bigfoot, as he'd wanted her to. But nobody believed her. She pulled the suit and the huge boots out of the closet they had shared, but this evidence was not enough. Some claimed to have spotted Bigfoot in Ohio and Indiana; some said he ranged as far north as Minnesota, south to the Carolinas. It was entirely possible that Bigfoot—the real one—was a migratory creature, experts opined. The joke had grown beyond them, and had a life of its own.

I have read of another joking husband, the Wakefield of Hawthorne's story, who, on a whim, abandons his wife and takes up residence in a nearby apartment. He continues the joke for twenty years, living unnoticed a street away from his former life. One afternoon, caught by a sudden storm, Wakefield blusters in his old door, returning to his wife and comfortable fireside. How she reacts to his sudden return we are not told. She had, of course, long thought herself a widow, as in practical fact she was.

Bigfoot's widow has an inverted situation. Instead of a husband who makes a joke of a twenty-years' disappearance—but lives—she has the memory of a husband whom no one will let die.

I wonder if she stops short when she sees the tabloid photos. Does it seem possible to hope that he lives, somewhere, that some quick-footed soul captured his shadow on film? He would seem nearer then—not a husband, quite, but maybe a neighbor. Someone to carry out the domestic transaction of borrow and lend, a twist of parsley, an egg passed warm from palm to palm. Close enough to meet, sometimes, so that even if changed, he wouldn't be a stranger. His place in the bed cool but waiting. Perhaps she thinks, *This could be some kind of test.* She imagines the wry smile on his face when he blows in the door on a rainy afternoon, pictures him slowly walking the world on those wide, solid feet, wrapped in a warm something she made, as she waits through the long years, tired, hoping he could be more cruel than she ever dreamed possible.

Gymnast

I would silence the announcers, babbling blowhards with muscles like unraveled yarn, their only aches come from too long
sitting, men who use talk like spray paint or cheaply made chisels, smearing and hacking what is well formed, solid, strong,
not theirs.

I would sprint the gym's dusty perimeter, yanking cord from
socket, killing the racket of "Malagueña" laid over with "Für
Elise" laid over with Sousa. One routine at a time, please. And
I would line up the coaches and lead them outside, pull them
out the open door into the bright rectangle of light as they,
hoarse, yell still their encouragement and blame.

Only this: the smack of feet on the mat, hand claps and a
cloud of chalk, the bar groaning with the body's flung weight.
For this is an affair of the body. If the body swings too far, it
will crumple to the mat. If the body is not strong enough, the
hands will release without the mind's consent. It is not a matter
of mind but of flesh, and it is not easy. Force the spine straight
and pull with the belly, legs together, twist and pivot and grip—
one hand shifting and the callused palm rubbing dry against
the bar—and as the body swings upward, ceiling rafters slide
smoothly down the wall to the floor and back up the wall to the
ceiling again, and at the last second the hands release the bar,
the wind nobody else hears blanks all other sound, legs tuck
and torso spins, heel and calf take the jolt of dismount: an electric bolt rising from the ground. Done. Watchers grow dizzy
by routine's end. Newly drunk, they tip in their seats, willing
themselves to fall.

I am smitten by the Russian gymnast Svetlana Khorkina,
smitten by the passion that looks like rage on her untranslatable

face. The sportscasters mock her look of fierce determination. Probably she terrifies them. They replay scenes from a past meet; over and over, the Svetlana of four years ago twists off the vault and into the air then crashes, midtuck, to the mat. Later the judges would discover that the vault had been set at the wrong height, a great controversy. But by the time they corrected the mistake, Svetlana's nerves were shot. Halfway through her uneven bars routine, her hands slipped and she fell to the floor, keeping her composure while on the mat but bursting into tears with her teammates and coach. The crew trained their cameras on her, on the tears streaking those high cheekbones.

Now she is twenty-five, old by the standards of the sport, and she knows this will be her last major meet. In an interview her translator says, *She says she wants to win as badly as she wants to mother her own child.* As Svetlana speaks, her eyes are calm, resolved. She accepts the contract's terms on faith; she will make her body a quill, a kiln, a highway; she will make her body do what her mind cannot imagine. She will create the idea made flesh, knowing it will hurt more than anything and cost her plenty. That is why I want her to win over the cherubic teen from Texas, equally determined, but by comparison a child herself.

Svetlana's turn. She tips her head to the judges, a formality. She thinks of what she must do, facing straight ahead, eyes on the vault, mouth set. Then from a dead stop she is running at top speed, arms pumping and legs flying at odd angles, for she is lean and long and her body, though strong, looks fragile, like a bundle of raw kindling. But with this body she can accomplish great things; with this narrow-hipped body (foot wrapped with tape, arch over instep over arch) she will scrawl rapid characters on the stale air of the gymnasium. Running, she points herself at the vault and grabs it, slams it, half a second of impact, arms down and legs straight in the air, and, twisting a tight corkscrew up and over and into a pike, she runs out of space and her feet hit the mat and from top speed she comes again to a dead stop, arms stretched above her head like the limbs of an elm, and again tips her head back to nod at the judges, inscrutable.

Does it matter that she doesn't win? That she comes in second to the teen from Texas? A week later, the Texan's grinning face is reproduced on French-fry wrappers at McDonald's the world over. But I can't shake the image of Svetlana, composed and calm, shoulders wrapped in the Russian flag, smiling serenely at her devotees.

And I wonder if she dreams sometimes, as I have, of her unconceived, those she traded for this, her pearl of great price. Not the medal; the medal is nothing. This: sole smacking mat, muscled arm's hard curve. Ephemeral in the end as an echo in an empty gym, a residue of dust suspended in the air. Her beautiful routine.

Who among us believes still in visions? I believe, for I have seen, do see, in dreams, my daughter. The electric shudder of child in body. The young are filaments of curled heat, glowing: things are not as we have been told.

Child, I dreamed you one morning. Your infant body pressing the crook of my arm felt real, solid as a bag of oranges. But when I turned your warm face to mine, you began your leaving, translucent scalp pulling in damp hair, eyelids fusing, body turning comma until you vanished. How can I speak to you, child who has never been?

Unmade daughter, if you would knot and swim within my body, know now that my first sacrifice has not been for you. Do not visit; do not make me turn you away.

Second-String

Stoat had worked for the carnival back then, doing a little bit of everything. Pulled levers, greased howling gears, evened legs with swiped shims, barked for the Free Shot and Whack-a-Cow, glowered in the Haunted Mill, fixed what broke. Something always broke. Hauled dripping bags of garbage to the dump, swung them over the fence. Once nearly toppled the Ferris Wheel (never set up on an incline). Once banged the bars in his cage and screamed: The Freak (pay your quarter! see the show!). And once, when the regular guy busted his arm, became the substitute human cannonball. "'Make yourself small,' he told me. 'Don't touch anything.'"

Summertime in South Carolina, and Stoat and I work together in the factory. I pack spark-plug shells, stacking good ones in cardboard boxes and spraying them with kerosene from a hissing silver can: a stay against rust. Bad parts, with ragged threads or blurred stamps, go in the red bin. There's something I like about the job. Being able to measure a good day's work by counting the number of wrapped boxes. The ache in my calves: standing eight hours, you earn your rest. The stink that clings to me (sweat, scorched machine oil, grease). People turn and stare in the grocery checkout. Stoat, a chip slinger though he knows arcane principles of electronics, shovels leftover steel from drop pans with a pitchfork when he has to. Given the chance, he'd rather talk. July heat rolls through the open shop door. It's broiling by nine in the morning; we start work at six. Outside, kudzu shimmers with green light, vines twining up telephone poles and choking pine trees, blanketing the old railroad tracks with leaves that shudder in the faint wind.

"Yeah, well, I never believed that cannonball guy," Stoat says, rubbing his stubbly jaw. "They were always playing tricks on me, thought I was stupid. I figured he was putting me on." Spindly, underfed, he wouldn't take up much room: probably why they'd chosen him. He'd crawled inside the cannon, smelled gunpowder, yes, and stale cloth, heat. "Braced myself," he says. "I just wanted to hold on."

The thing threw him, as it was meant to, over the staring crowd, bareback riders in snagged satin, goats with crumpled horns, skinny girls shaking tambourines. And the audience, like flowers tracking the sun, forgot their own faces to follow his. Looking down, he saw a boy in a jacket worn hard, leaking fill. A pleading woman clutched a man by the elbow. A family of four, each with the same broken-thumb nose. That was the first time.

In the days after that, Stoat did his routine again and again, keeping tabs on his other work after the show. In the tired, small hours: spliced wires, replaced sockets, lit his work with an old Coleman lantern. Millers fluttered to the ragged mantle, leaving their poor dust on the glass. Flattened cans on the midway picked up shine from his lamp and, further out, headlights. In the dirt parking lot, kids revved engines, shrieked onto the highway. Stoat taped wires, snipped copper. Mufflers faded to a smear, silence. And always the crickets throbbed.

"Put a cape on my neck and a helmet on my head," he says, "but that was just for show. So is the gunpowder, an effect, it's a spring on a platform that shoots you. Smacks you right in the butt. That first time gave me bruises all over. But once I got good, I pointed my arms in the air and flew," he says. "Just like a swan."

That's years ago. Here, in the factory, Stoat pulls a pocket-knife to dig in his palm after curls of brass and steel, works metal from his hand, sucks blood. Then the floor boss walks by, and Stoat, now an old man, picks up his pitchfork and heads for the next machine.

I can guess the rest:

Night after night, the hollow drumroll, a glaze of light—later, twists of wire, racing lights flashing on the deserted strip in what would be, by Monday, just another empty field between towns, passionflower clawing hard dirt, marquee listing past dates. Gone the goats and the popcorn machine, stubs ragged as yanked teeth, sawdust damp with drink. Milk buckets and softballs shoved in a truck bed. And Stoat himself arcing over another crowd, eyes watering from the wind, hoping to land in the net. The big tent poles swaying and pulling. Below, someone watching. Someone walking away.

Ave Maria Grotto

I imagine it this way: sun lifting over pine woods, crows calling, a woodpecker drumming on the monastery eaves. He's
awake already, kneeling beside his narrow bed; his joints pop
as he stands. Slowly he makes his way toward the workshop.
The dew's risen from the packed dirt path. How quickly a day
passes, and how little we manage to save.

A bag of cotton tick slumps on the workshop threshold.
Loosening the drawstring, he plunges his hand inside and
lifts out marbles, slick and cool. Ruby, rust, indigo drops, insides dabbled with caught air. Bright, wrinkled feathers (blue
jay, oriole) piercing clear cats' eyes. Opaque ones, striped yellow and black like a highway. He sets the bag down—it's heavy
for its size—and dips up another handful, milk glass, scrubbed
bone streaked with cinnamon. Cupping an outsized shooter in
his wrinkled palm, he's tempted to save the prettiest for some
future use. But he resists this impulse as miserly and pours the
marbles from his hand back into the bag. They click as they
fall, the sound sharp as an overheard complaint. He pulls the
drawstring tight.

All gifts are honorable, but to him this one seems more so.
He imagines the child who left it for him, riding with his parents to the monastery, the nubby wheat-colored carpet and stale
smell in the back seat, the running seam marking the backs of
his legs. He helped his father unload the bags of things they
had no more use for while his mother waited, window rolled
down, slapping a mosquito. The other bags hold the usual
detritus of an American postwar family: leftover honeycombs

from some tiling project, a cracked vase, soup spoons discarded when a new pattern came. But the marbles are different; Joseph knows it. The boy gave up something he loved. Perhaps. Or else he disobeyed, and his parents exacted this self-denial as payment. Or someone teased him for playing still with children's toys. Or he had simply grown up and left home: the boy could well be a soldier in Korea, his parents cleaning the house, worrying away the hours.

Joseph had known when he left—long ago, a boy of fourteen—that there would be no returning. Had he had a choice? But God had been good. In the spindly pine woods of northeastern Alabama, clear-cut and slowly growing back, he saw traces of the Black Forest his parents had once taken him to see. Shortly after his arrival at the monastery, the abbot had put him to work in the physical plant, where he learned to tighten loose knobs, wrap frayed wires, make sturdy the wobbling leg. It was good work—Christ himself had been a carpenter—and he liked the routine of the Benedictine day, always had. The quiet breathing of his brothers at morning prayer, smell of roasting potatoes from the kitchen, pattern of call and response, cicadas rattling through the hot afternoon. It had become a home for him. And yet.

Sometimes, in the workshop, newly useless pieces confronted him—stripped screws, wood scraps, broken tiles—junk made so by a careless stroke of his own, or simple exhaustion of the material. And he could not bear to throw them out. He dropped them into empty food-service cans and they accumulated, like small change, over time. It was a strange thing for a Benedictine to be a pack rat, and occasionally he puzzled over what to do with the junk. There could be no truly worthless thing; perhaps, he thought, it was a problem of transposing something into its next place of service. Who would mar a clear-grained plank with a rusty nail? Yet the cook sometimes dropped a nail into a pot of beans for the iron, imparting strength to the eaters' bones.

In his mind he climbed again the tier of four steps, and his father pushed open one of the great Gothic doors. Inside it was dim, the air fragrant with faded incense, fir boughs, and the medicinal-smelling wax the sexton used to polish the floors. He saw the tall windows, eight on either side of the nave, windows he had counted again and again as a child, and he remembered the colored light that used to glide along the walls, in August gilding or bluing the faces of worshipers, in December burning high and cold on the cobwebbed clerestory.

And so it started, merely a whim, a project to fill the evening hour between compline and sleep. With the scraps that cluttered the shop he would model the church of his baptism. He framed it with leftover boards, marking lines with a flat pencil, tearing a neat seam with the saw blade. With a practiced angle of the wrist, he rasped the edges smooth. The tall windows he filled with painted Nehi bottle fragments; the steeply pitched roof he fashioned from chips of red cedar, toenailing each in place. Last, he dipped a narrow brush into a tin of white paint and lettered a sign: *Cathedral, Landshut Bavaria, My Home.*

He had never thought of himself as homesick, but after he finished that building sleep came more easily. Perhaps, he thought, it was due simply to his additional hour's labor. He did not know if the church had survived the second war; dreams came to him (flaming rafters crashing to the floor, kindling the pews' rubbed wood; a smoke-blackened ruin hulked in the town square). But more often, lately, he didn't dream at all, and was thankful for that. The model church, draped with an oilcloth, stood in an unused corner of the workshop. It had taken him months to finish, and he did not think of making more.

But overnight, it seemed, things broke more easily, and the cans of junk he'd emptied refilled. Material cried out for a use. And so, almost out of habit, he began working on another project, a model of historic Jerusalem. One evening he looked up, startled, to see the abbot peering into the workshop door. He showed him pages he'd torn from a magazine and tacked to a board, explained the supports that would frame Solomon's temple, lifted the corner of the oilcloth. The abbot, not a man given to unconsidered opinions, examined these things in silence, then draped the cloth as it had been and let himself out, shutting the door behind him. A few days later he took Joseph aside and gave his approval for the work to continue, even allowing him an hour out of his daily duties to make his models. When he finished Jerusalem, four of the brothers slipped lengths of rope underneath and carried it to a flat spot beneath some skinny pines. Landshut Cathedral they placed nearby. In this way, the work he had done in his spare hours was made public.

Gradually he was excused from other duties in order to work on his models, which became a local attraction. The abbot encouraged the people of the town to donate their castoffs for building materials. *When they participate in the work, they move closer to God,* he said. *They give what they can spare.* Joseph said nothing, sifting through piles of junk.

And though he tried to resist it, sometimes resentment rose in him when he walked in the foggy morning to the workshop door and saw what the townspeople had left for him. At night, always at night, they left things they would be ashamed to own in the day. Blouses worn to translucence, too thin even for dust rags, or stacks of rotten newspapers; once a dead muskrat, a Singer sewing machine, finish flaked down to raw metal, works rusted solid. He took to wearing canvas gloves after gashing his hand on a broken milk bottle. Did they credit him with transformative powers? He could not make things new.

So he loved more the unseen givers who left things that were still beautiful: the sack of marbles, a box of green Irish fishing floats packed in crisp tissue paper, a hoe's smooth wooden handle, a copper pan polished in concentric circles so that it shone. He imagined the giver with a handful of chalk powder and a damp rag, falling into reverie (girlhood, an hour at the lake) as afternoon lengthened into evening and the copper grew bright under her hands.

Time passed, and with his hands and the junk of his midden pile he made places he had never seen, working from postcards and magazine clips: the Leaning Tower and St. Peter's, the Alamo and the Statue of Liberty, Lourdes, San Marco, a graveyard in Korea with tiny white crosses for the local boys buried there. Parents came, standing silently by the spot. And when he died in 1961, an old man and full of years, his brothers buried him in the monastery plot, not far from the wooded valley, formerly a quarry, he had filled with miniatures. Today, if Cullman's known for anything, it's for the hobby of Brother Joseph Zoettl, a man with a hunch in his back, who lived long in a land not his own and about whom little is known: I piece this together from fragments. Tourists walk up and down the paths, looking at the child-height buildings, marveling at his patience. I was among them, there on a lark—"See the buildings made of toilet-bowl floats and costume jewelry!"—but unable to shake a deeper feeling.

I think how the women of my family saved scraps of outgrown clothing, stitching them together with doubled thread to warm our sleep. How my mother, at the end of the season, drives to the local tomato farm, picks bag after bag of ten-cent-a-pound tomatoes, scrubs, blanches, peels, and slices them, filling clean wide-mouth Masons with red pulp and sealing them well. Through her alchemy we have August's tomatoes in January, some years a hundred quarts' worth. Each jar we empty she scours and bleaches and puts away in the canning closet. There is honor in hard use—well I know it, and so did this man, fitting piece to piece, filling gaps with a mortar of sand and silt, rich with the leavings of Alabama and all the lands northward.

I think, too, of exile, how this man left his home when he was just a boy, about the age Christ would have been when he argued with the rabbis in the temple. He must have known, even then, that there would be no returning for him. He did the best, the most useful, work that he could. When he was past the middle years of his quiet life, he built a model of the church he attended as a boy, and painted the words *Landshut, Bavaria, My Home.* Exile seems part of the biblical life, in these times as in former ones. On their own, these things—thrift, love of home—would be enough. And yet. There is something more.

In sixteenth-century Italy, painters' patrons left them chunks of precious lapis lazuli, the ultimate gift: at the time, lapis was more costly than gold. Imagine a workshop, a master and his apprentices preparing a wall for a fresco, bags of chalk powder and lime, tin pails of water, all the plaster-making tools, paddles. On the appointed day the master himself—he would trust this job to no one—wraps an indigo stone in linen, places the bundle on the bench, brings the mallet down, hard, then raises the hammer and hits it again. Setting the mallet aside, he lifts the bundle, fingering the broken pieces, then shunts the fragments into a hard stone bowl and grinds the pestle, leaning hard. He shouts at an underling to scour the floor for chips of blue, reminding him he'll be whipped well if he takes so much as a splinter for himself. *This blue is given to God's glory,* he says, *this blue is to atone for the sins of the Medici.* Everyone laughs at that. And as the boy works a sliver of lapis from between two floor tiles and drops it quick under the scarred pestle, the master says, *Boys, today we make our heaven.*

They did their work well; my eyes have seen the proof, San Miniato's sapphire ceiling still the same rich shade, its hammered -gold stars gleaming in the shadowy vault. And I think that fresco painter, his name lost now, must have felt, then, like the wealthiest man in the province as he broke something so costly. He did what no duke could, as with muscled arm and skill, he made a new sky, closer to earth. Perhaps he thought, as he worked, of that old verse in Jeremiah: *What has straw in common with wheat? Is not my word like fire, says the Lord, and like a hammer that breaks a rock in pieces?* Then it fit; he understood. Only what's broken can fully be used. Nothing too humble; nothing too good.

Even on Sundays

My mother told this story about her grandparents:

Moore kept his farm a showplace by working himself and his family hard, even on Sundays. His white barn towered above the surrounding fields, the tin-roofed farmhouse, and his wife's neat peony-edged garden. Inside the barn, everything had its place. Hoes and rakes hung by leather thongs, and the joints of the trailer were supple with grease. Even in the chicken house not a shingle was loose, and the cleats of its ramp were nailed down tight. Every morning his wife gathered the eggs she would use that day from beneath the hens' warm rumps.

He must have been near the farmhouse when the stroke hit, because she found him right away. Maybe he was eating lunch at the long table, listening to the radio news; a strange light came into his eyes and he stiffened, then fell out of his chair, knife and fork clattering to the ground. The radio announcer murmured on, relating the morning's farm market report.

So it became her job to care for him. She bent over the bed and lifted the body grown frail from disuse, tipped mush into his mouth and wiped his chin. She heated water on the stove for shaving, pulled his skin taut with her thumb, and drew the blade over the day's rasping growth. She bent his arms and guided them into sleeves, cut his nails, stroked his once-calloused palms. She pushed his squeaking hospital bed from room to room to give him change of scene. (She had ordered the doors widened especially for this purpose, had had a picture window cut in a wall.) So passed three years.

After he died she wrote my mother a letter. *This isn't living. Living was walking through the cornfields with Ernest.* That was 1967. She stayed alone until her death, twenty-one years later.

We drove slowly past the old farmhouse as my mother spoke, and I imagined them as they must have been, my great-grandparents, his work-roughened hands parting the waist-high leaves, the cornstalks pulling at her skirts. Their backs to us. Walking toward the fence line, the green smell of plants and damp earth pressing the soles of their feet. Her hair pulled tightly back in a knot. Him tall, a little stooped, his hair thinning at the crown, neck tanned and speckled from the sun. Maybe I've got it wrong. But maybe when she remembered her happiness it looked like this: his known face turning aside to examine the corn as the reclining summer sun turned the sky pink behind him, his hands brushing the leaves. She tended him as he'd tended the ground and what grew there, never sparing a day; not for profit or pride, but because this was the work she knew.

Plenty

I.

At midday the sky darkened, and the men and women felt in their bones a deep, susurrant sound, throaty like far thunder but lasting, a body's hurried heartbeat made loud enough for all to hear. The cat cried, the children lit out. Bits of straw danced in the cowshed. The men grabbed their guns, bags of shot. Meat rained down on the tenant farm, where they measured meals by mouthfuls, and someone's job it was to pluck the pinfeathers. The dark meat tasted of ashes. They ate it all and pounded the thin bones for marrow.

Imagine a vast deciduous forest stretching from the Mississippi to the Atlantic. Imagine a single tree in that forest, a chestnut, with a thick trunk and sawblade-edged leaves. Birds build their twiggy nests in its forks. The nests look careless, thrown together, and they stud the tree, several dozen at least, each containing a lone egg. Drab birds perch on the nests, gather grasses, nuts. The undersides of their wings flash white in flight. Settled on the nest, they blend with the grayish tan of the chestnut bark, with the fallen leaf litter on the ground beneath them. Copper blooms at the throat. There is nothing remarkable about these birds, except that they are so many. Nests without number dot the tree next to our chestnut, and the tree next to that, and the next. One afternoon, a stout hickory splits beneath the weight of the nests burdening it. The trunk gives with a great crack, then a crashing as the nests fall, a startled, exclamatory cooing. Smashed eggshells lie crumpled on the broken sticks. A dark eyespot dots one yolk, drying slowly in the morning sun.

There is nothing at all remarkable about this bird, except that it is the passenger pigeon, and at this point in its history —shortly before its catastrophic decline—it is the most abundant land bird in all of North America. It travels in flocks of a million or more, seeking hard, rich things—chestnuts, beechnuts, acorns—things wanting a good crack. It seems always "in passage," never lingering long, building its risky roost and laying a single egg, counting on the numbers of its kin to keep up the species.

Of course, both the great deciduous forest of the east and the passenger pigeon that haunted it are gone now. In the early twentieth century, blight killed all of the American chestnut trees. All of them. I have seen a young chestnut, just head-high, leafing out in an Appalachian May. Blight will strangle its roots and burn its leaves before it passes twenty summers. The passenger pigeon, with its immense flocks, must have seemed inexhaustible, everlasting, common as a Tuesday. A combination of clear-cutting, railroads, and overshooting killed the passenger pigeon. The last one, a female, died in a Cincinnati zoo in 1914.

The passenger pigeons' red feet are wired to the bough. I have visited often their alcove in the quiet museum of natural history. They are remarkable not for their appearance—only the sparrow could be less flashy—but for their story, the breakneck velocity of their decline. Male and female are—were—almost identical, the male's breast slightly brighter, the color of toasted wheat bread. The museum was fortunate indeed to get these skins, and I wonder if these were among the last of their kind. Male and female, juvenile and adult, they look nearly alike to me. I could not have told them apart in the field. In fact, though I have studied the passenger pigeon, I can't claim to know it. Poor farmers a century ago knew the bird, had tasted its flesh. Like the Israelites in the desert, food rained down from heaven. They took this concession from the Lord, one of the few they had the chance to claim.

2.

The hermit had lived in a cabin of his own making, deep in the woods, for as long as anyone could remember. Sometimes deer hunters spotted him, but only sometimes. When my father was a boy, hunting rats for bounty, he had seen the old hermit. "In the old corncrib," Dad said, "a good place to hunt rats. Took a stick to poke with, startle the ones the snakes didn't catch. Plenty rats for all of us, snakes and boys. I was cutting the tail off one, putting it in my bag to take to the extension agent, when I looked up and saw the old man. Standing in the open corncrib door. He didn't say a word, didn't say 'Get up and get on,' though he must have thought it. After a while he left. They say the old man murdered his only son, but I don't believe that. You know the police never found a body, just the kid's car, parked in the grass along the road."

The hermit lived on what he could find, or so we guessed. Sometimes in winter we'd smell wood smoke; he was keeping warm. Did he hunt game, did he fish Black Pond in summer? Did he plant potatoes near his house, as we did? We never knew anything for sure. One summer the hermit died from eating too many wild blackberries. Someone found him stumbling along the county road and tried to take him to the hospital. He died on the way. Blocked bowel, the doctors said. Who knew how long it had been troubling him?

How long did it take for the bough to snap, finally, under his weight, the bundle of all he carried? I think he felt himself grow heavy, pulled down by memories of his life as a young man, the wife he once had, the way she slept her brittle sleep. Deer stotting through the woods, the sharp smell of gunpowder, how carefully he cut their throats. He sank slowly into the earth, the soles of his feet pressing the humus more heavily than before, then in to his ankles, gradually, the way a man steps into a gently sloping lake. It grows deep, so deep, but not right away. Up to his shins—the woods weighing him down now, the hawk he once saw with a snake hanging from its beak, the rusty barbed wire the hickory swallowed—up to his knees, and then he fell in. He must have felt immortal at the end. The last heir of a great tribe.

Alcott in Concord

Amos Bronson Alcott was Louisa May's father and, by most accounts, something of a crank. He used to sit along the Concord Road with a basket of apples, waiting for passersby; when he saw a traveler, he'd call out, offering to trade an apple for a conversation. Were people flattered, confused, wary? What did he hope to gain?

It's a little like the phenomenon of the gam, which Ishmael explains in *Moby-Dick*. When ships met on the high, lonesome seas, they'd pull near each other and take time to exchange news and letters. Maybe Alcott, marooned in his brilliant village, hungered for the thrill of an unfamiliar face, news from elsewhere. Or maybe Alcott's urge is related to Benjamin Franklin's drive toward self-betterment: education on the cheap, just an apple and a moment of your time. An apple exchanged for a stranger's knowledge sounds familiar, apocryphal. Would that make it less true?

Late one winter, about this time of year, I found myself in Concord on a raw afternoon, trudging along the busy turnpike, trying to get to Walden Pond. I kept my head down, walking over shattered ruby taillights, cigarette butts, crushed cans, a bent license plate. Salt-rimed transfer trucks blasted past in gusts of cold air. I hummed Lyle Lovett songs to keep my spirits up, and the only sign I could find that someone had walked that way before was a pair of old shoe prints in the sand. How grateful I was to see them. *Make me the cup of strength to suffering souls*, Episcopalians pray. You never know what your cup of strength might look like.

Twice a year and always alone, I used to make the thousand-mile drive from Houston to South Carolina. How many times during those long drives did I stop in a diner and order something—a patty melt, a cup of coffee—not because I was hungry, but because I needed to hear people talking? I remember a boy's narrow shoulders as he bent over the deep cookstove. Eyes on something else, he reached for the steel dipper of oil, or a bucket of half-frozen hash browns. I loved watching him work. The wire basket of eggs above his head, and the finger-marked chrome toaster reflecting his grasping hand. If he noticed me, he didn't show it.

Why did Alcott do it? The impulse seems generous at first; maybe he hoped to welcome strangers to his town with a kindness. But it's self-interested, too. Conversation as transaction. *Just talk to me. I'll pay.*

▪ ▪ ▪

A grasshopper blunders into a spiderweb, snagging a leg, and tugs fruitlessly at the silk. Calmly, the spider drops to where the snared insect struggles, secures it with a few bights of silk, then rolls it rapidly into a bundle, spindling it into a white skein as the doomed creature's legs shiver and work. Dark tobacco juice stains the shroud. She slips in her fangs, then tacks and weaves her way back to web's center to wait.

Alcott's watched the whole lopsided struggle, mildly interested. A basket of wrinkled apples rests by his side, perfuming the air with decay. Bright leaves twist in the wind. It won't be long, he knows, before he'll brush snow from this very spot.

Sometimes he thinks he could wait right here, as day sinks into night, leaves dulling then dropping, cased in ice, as tracks mar the first heavy snow and deer strip bark from young willow trees. Wait as wind carves the snow into dunes, scouring down to bare dirt in the low places, apples deflate into limp puddles spiky with mold, and the earth slowly turns back to warmth. He could wait through all that, melting snow dropping from the brim of his crumpled hat; he could wait, eyes flicking from side to side. Steel-gray hair reaching farther down his collar, fingernails growing articulate as talons. He could wait. For someone to talk to.

To Hear Her Tell It

Avery Island, Louisiana. 1870?

He needed a project, she could see that. She had enough to do to keep the family alive, managing the stringy chickens, grubbing vegetables from the sand, finding enough to pay the few servants who'd stayed. Yes, her hands found abundant work. He was different. After his bank collapsed, he had no job; he blamed the war, but in truth the bank would have foundered in any event, and the shots on Fort Sumter merely hastened the inevitable. She was the one to suggest he go to the city. A trip might put things right.

She'd heard him tell the story enough times to piece together how it must have been. He arranged to meet some friends in a public house in the Quarter, hoping to find work, but they were all talk and no prospects. He crushed his disappointment in the usual ways; being neither blind nor stupid, she could guess what they were. Time passed in a hazy string of hours, smoke and shrimp, rum and dark-haired women. He didn't remember how the young soldier—lucky bastard, to have lived through it—wound up at their table, but by night's end, he'd found himself walking the cobblestone streets by his side, listening to him talk about the chances awaiting the ambitious Southern man. When the soldier pressed something into his palm, she knew it wouldn't have occurred to him to pull away. He closed his fingers over the muslin-wrapped packet, slid his hand in his pocket. The soldier took his leave and stepped down a side alley. When the man walked off the train the following day, he was full of excitement—she could see possibility in his face—but he didn't seem to know the exact reason.

Upstairs in his study, he closed the heavy oaken door behind him. He unwrapped the packet and a clutch of yellow seeds, flat and circular, fell out; he pondered what to do. Did the seeds matter enough to plant, or should he simply throw them away? He'd made financial decisions that affected the lives of hundreds of wealthy Louisianans; wasn't it beneath him to till the earth, even in the smallest capacity? He sat in his study, looking out the window at the Gulf, glittering in the noonday sun. A sheaf of papers rested on the corner of the polished desk, papers he wasn't ready to think about: bills, tax notices, more bills. Beneath the surface of the island lay his wife's dowry, a salt mine, which Confederate troops had made plentiful use of during the war. Their officers paid a fair price in notes backed by the full authority of the Confederate States of America. A lower drawer of the desk was full of the neatly stacked and banded notes. For all they were worth he might as well have thrown them in the Gulf.

A change of scene might help him think. Pushing away from his desk, he strode down the stairs with more authority than she'd seen in him in a long time. Outside, he knelt in a corner of the vegetable garden and broke clods of the gray, sandy soil in his hands, letting it fall damply to the ground. With his thick fingers, pale from shaded living, he poked divots in the sand and dropped a few seeds in each. After covering them, he carried a bucket of brackish water from the well and poured it over his little plot. From the cook he demanded a few yards of kitchen twine: he looked so strange, his sweaty forehead plastered with hair, blotched face streaming, she dared not ask him why. He staked the garden's four corners with kindling and wrapped twine around each stake.

Morning and evening for days to come, she watched him lug buckets from the well. Soon three parallel lines of green sprouted in the sandy gumbo. Days passed, and the young plants grew oval leaves, flowers budded and bloomed, and, after the shriveled blooms dropped, shiny peppers filled out in little green fingers. By this time the pepper plants had become his obsession—his project, the thing for which she had prayed. If the plants needed water three times a day, he hauled the water. If he found a beetle or grub on the leaves, he crushed it between two fingers, absently wiping his hands on his trousers. One hot afternoon a storm boiled up, as it often does here, wind whipping the Gulf into white breakers and tossing the branches of the spreading oaks. Rushing into his chamber, he pulled a sheet from the bed and tore it into strips, running outside, gusts of wind sending leaves and broken wood flying across the yard. Quickly he tented the plants, tying the linen tight as lightning cracked over the water and the sky churned. Lying on the ground, muddy, disheveled, he would have stayed out there during the whole squall if she had allowed it; standing on the porch, she pleaded with him to come in, the children (had they made children together?) clinging to her skirts and wailing.

By month's end the summer sun had ripened the peppers, and he began the harvest. Some he dried or kept for seed, others he ate out of hand, testing the heat of shades ranging from orange to crimson to a dark, bruised purple. As he worked in the tool shed, inspiration struck. He measured salt from the mine into a bowl, added minced pepper and a little water, and stirred it well. He poured the soup into a clean bottle and capped it tightly, and as she passed through the shed, hunting a hoe to tend the squash, she heard him mutter calculations, how many rows he'd plant next season, and next. In this way, Tabasco sauce began on Avery Island, above the underground salt mine that formed the basis of his dwindling wealth.

To hear him tell it, that's the end of the story; he's the hero of a fairy-tale fortune, and the soldier's a wandering wise man who gave him the seeds. (Or traded them, but for what? In those times, as now, nothing was given freely.) But I don't think that's all.

I went on the Tabasco factory tour and heard the spiel. The guide mentioned the founder's wife in terms of her dowry, nothing more. But someone kept the plantation scraping by while he was taking trips to New Orleans. She gets no credit; here's the way I see it.

He was a man to whom others gave things. She gave him soil to build his garden and water to dampen the shoots, gave him salt from her mine to make the sauce of his famously simple discovery. (Listen, everything they grew tasted of salt, every leaf crusted with white.) I wonder if she begrudged him anything.

But when he claimed that stars aligned to make him prosper, know she aligned them. Her hands pressed rail fare into his palms; her hands scrubbed and mended. She worked so hard that he closed his eyes to it, and saw neither her nor her labor. She sheltered him lest he perish like a wind-broke stalk. And then one night he met a soldier on a rain-slicked street. Reckon this to her account, and I will answer for it: the work he did was what she prepared him to do.

Barefoot in a Borrowed Corset

SPELUNKER[1]

Some cave naked for fear of contaminating the water they mean to study.

Stripping quickly in the pale light of the cave's opening chamber, she tucks her bundle of clothing behind a stone, shoulders her pack, and steps into darkness.

As the passage twists and descends, her light illuminates the step ahead of her.[2] Then the next. She takes each pace as it comes, easing between tight places, scratching her thighs on limestone outcrops. The air tastes thick, like last season's potatoes. Then she smells water.

She steps into the lake with a gasp; the cold's always a shock. In this first chamber, a great cavern ringed with dripping stalactites, she strokes confidently through the water; it's several stories deep, she knows, but so clear the bottom seems just out of reach. She floats into a narrow defile, mineral-rich water wrinkling her fingertips, whitening pared nails. The bright cone of her miner's light picks out the curling print of a fossil ammonite. She hauls herself onto a boulder and maps her path on damp graph paper, noting the fossils and formations she's

---

[1]After reading, in a borrowed house, a stranger's *National Geographic*.
[2]On the longest night of the year, a bulb burns in the narrow kitchen, the stove's four small cataracts mouth their patient sighs, and the burner leaps into flame when breathed upon. And this is a stay against darkness, the voice of a kettle stretching into thin song. Later, awake, I lie beside him, my arm pressing his back's seam. He sleeps softly; I am trying to learn this. Instead, I listen as the old accordion radiator rills and knocks.

seen, the smoky script of candle-writing on an overhanging ledge near the entrance. A stream of bats pours down the ceiling above her; it must be dusk, time for them to feed.

She drinks bottled protein shakes, relieves herself in a jar, washes perfunctorily with cloths stashed in her pack. She is careful because of the things she sees[3] and those she does not.[4] She spends a string of silky hours in darkness,[5] their passing marked by the phosphorescent glow of her waterproof wristwatch.

When she steps out of the water, her feet leave a trail of firm prints that nobody will ever see. Surfacing in the sun's blinding spray, naked as a newborn, what does she say? That she had tried to cleanse herself like a priest or a surgeon,[6] had tried not to befoul the place; had tried to see what was there so she could tell the others, the ones too afraid to go.

MUSEUM GOER

Ten years ago, semester abroad, and my art-history class went to Milan to see *The Last Supper*. Our professor[7] told us about the technique da Vinci had tried, painting on dry plaster instead of damp so that he could touch up the colors, make the scene more lifelike. He got the effect he wanted, but at a cost; the paint began to peel shortly after he finished, and that was five hundred years ago.[8]

---

[3]Pale amphibians with blood-bright gills and useless eyespots.
[4]Slips squiggling through the water.
[5]Once, on a cave tour, I heard a guide claim that a human, if trapped in a cave with no flashlight, would go blind in two weeks from the strain of searching for light where none can be.
[6]Or museum goer.
[7]Of whom the studio art prof said, incredulously, *She works five days a week!*
[8]Thus the painting's fragility calls attention to its mortality.

As I stood in line, waiting my turn with the fresco, I felt as though I were intruding on a private moment, a mere acquaintance visiting someone gravely ill; I tried not to take up much space. When my turn came, I stepped into a small chamber, and glass doors tightly sealed the entrance and exit. Then a series of powerful fans roared to life, yanking at my clothes and blasting my hair, making my eyes water. A recorded voice informed me that this was the cleansing room; the fans were supposed to shake off street dust, to protect the delicate painting. When the fans clicked off, it seemed very quiet; the door slid open, and I walked into the room that contained the painting. I looked at it for the prescribed number of minutes, and the docent herded me out.

When I think of the painting now, I barely remember the flaking paint, the mastery of one-point perspective, the expression on Christ's face—are his eyes downcast or raised? It's the cleansing room I think of, with its bag of winds that made me feel more contaminated somehow than I had before, walking down the street in the yellow sun, watching pigeons (*filthy birds,* my mother says) wheel through the air.

Altar Guild

At Trinity Church in Houston, I served on the altar guild with a group of capable, particular Texas ladies. We took turns gathering the communion things after service, washing them, and putting them away: chalice, pitcher, bowl. We bought linens from a Spanish convent, and I thought of the nuns while I presoaked the stained napkins; Episcopalian ladies could not be prevailed upon to blot their lipstick before approaching the rail.

I scrubbed the linen with a bar of honey-colored glycerin soap we kept for just that purpose; when the lipstick and dark wine lifted, I draped the dripping squares over the drying rack.

Every week, we washed the blood of Christ from the rim of the common cup, wiped clean the print of many lips. If any fragments of body were left over, we took them outside and laid them on the grass.

But I confess: I have gone to work in God's scullery still damp with love, have calculated the cost of the heavy sterling chalices, their insides washed with gold. Lust and greed. I have shut my ears, unrepentant. I have scrubbed with dirty hands.[9]

NAAMAN, AILING[10]

I learned the story of Naaman in Sunday school: Naaman the Syrian was a military man, good at what he did, expert at sensing weakness and pressing advantage; he almost always won. Because of this, Naaman owned many changes of clothing and casks of oil, wives and concubines and the children they bore him, menservants and maidservants and cattle and he-asses. He also had leprosy, which nothing could cure.

Naaman had taken a Hebrew servant girl during a skirmish. He gave her to one of his wives, maybe one who'd complained of feeling slighted, maybe a favorite. One day the servant saw him dressing, the tunic fallen open to reveal discolored, pebbly skin on his forearms, and he turned away, shamed. Shaking, he roared, *Get out of here!*

---

[9]And yet. I think of the cups I made with slick clay and potter's wheel, shapes forming wet under the press of my hand and the smooth slide of fingers. When they dried I fired them in the kiln. After I brought them home, they clicked from the heat slowly escaping them. I slept shallowly then, and sometimes the ticking pots woke me. They seemed alive. Companionable. I'd walk back to my rented room, pant legs stiff with dried mud, fingertips scoured and glowing. Clean, clean, with my pared nails and ringless fingers. Fingerprinted clay and mud-slipped hands. *Clay is a very forgiving material,* one of the experienced potters told me.

[10]2 Kings 5:1–14.

That night the girl spoke to her mistress. *He should go to the prophet of my people, in Samaria,* the servant girl said. *Elisha. He would know how to cure my lord.*

So he went to this Elisha, and the man wouldn't even meet with him. A messenger came out to say, *Wash seven times in the Jordan, and your skin will be as that of a little child.*

Naaman stared at the messenger, incredulous. Obviously the man meant to insult him. The Jordan was filthy, and besides, it was strange to him. There were any number of superior rivers back home where he could have washed, saving himself the trip. He kicked his horse in the side, and a rooster tail of dust rose from the dry path as he rode away, blind with anger. He was a powerful man. And yet there was this sickness he could not order away, that made people despise him. Maybe this was how he had been able to wrangle such power from others; his weakness (how he hated it) showed him how to exploit theirs.

Then one of his men[11] rode up to him, someone bold enough to speak to Naaman when he was in such a thunder. Dared to say, *If the prophet had asked a hard thing, you would have done it. Why not this?*

Why not this? The Jordan was close at hand; he could smell the dank water.

Why not this? And prove that prophet a fakir.

Why not this? He had come so far already.

Dismounting, he gave the lead rope to a servant. Heat rose off the stones. The tilting sun flashed on the water as he walked to the river, where he loosed his belt, unbound his tunic, squatted to pick at the knots securing his sandals. Stood there naked, surrounded by drying dung, buzzing flies at feed. Did he bark at his men to look the other way, or was that already

---

[11]A brother?

their habit? Did he say, *Look at me; this is what it is to be mortal*, and mock the ones who flinched?

He stepped into the spit-warm water, arms half-raised for balance, and stared across the river, narrowing his eyes against the glare. Silt swirled around his feet, and he sank a little in the muck. He moved in up to the knees, the firm, battle-scarred flanks, his sex floating on the water, and then he dipped himself for the first time into the cave of damp clay the river had become. Surfacing, he shook water from his eyes. He raised his arms out of the river and watched rivulets of water run down the scabbed skin, slicking the hairs, staining his nails. He stepped out further, the water chest deep now. He couldn't hear the rustling leaves of trees whose names he didn't know, or the cry of the strange birds flying overhead—only the sound of rushing water, a river of mud. He dropped to his knees, feeling the current knock him off his feet momentarily, and then flexed, surfaced, spouting. The second time. Under again, into the opaque water, and up, the current pulling at him, standing there alone; again, and a slick fish brushed his chest, startling him. Standing in the water, watching the sun lowering toward the western horizon, he sank into the river, tasted earth, and thought of woman, body's damp flavor. A cold patch of water hit him and passed on. Should he do anything different for the last time? Did it matter? Hypnotic, this rising and falling, sevenfold washing. He turned to the near bank, where his men still waited, and as he stepped out he felt water sloughing him, the dry air wicking his skin. Ran his hands through his dripping hair, picked out a twig, tasted grit. Shook himself.

One of the lads turned and saw his grimy captain naked, bedraggled, cleansed.

Naaman the Syrian looked at himself. Pulled the skin on his arm and saw it snap back, healthy. For once in his life, had nothing to say.

CALDERA

It's a blue so startling you want to gorge yourself on it, gaze at it until (like an idea) you can't see it anymore. Crater Lake, the deepest lake in the United States, may be one of the purest; its waters come from springs and snowmelt, not creeks, so there's no till. Lapis, cobalt, midnight blue. Even at the lake's deepest point,[12] a little light still filters through. Navy soup in a gray bowl.

But only blue from a distance, of course. On a hot August day, I hiked down the steep path to the water's edge, peeled off shoes and socks, and jumped in. What had been blue turned clear as quartz, and it was so cold (thirty-seven degrees) that it knocked out my air.[13] But I wanted this. I stroked past the underwater boulders near the shore and opened my eyes as the bottom fell away and the water bore me up. I floated there as long as I could stand it, thinking of the mikvah, Jewish ritual bath,[14] how the bather must be completely naked, no earrings or contact lenses, nails unpolished and hair unbound. I needed that cold swim on that hot day, have needed the memory of it many times since. Needed to shake off the dust. Long ago, a great explosion formed the lake. It had been a classic cinder cone before. This is what scientists think; we can't know for certain.

---

[12] 1,932 feet; the same year FDR was elected to his first term.

[13] *Point your arms above your head, honey, like you're a diver,* she said, helping me into the wedding dress. Seed pearls were strewn on the boutique's camel-colored carpet, like shells at the beach. She was practiced in this, fitting expensive gowns to the bodies of other women. I was a novice, barefoot in a borrowed corset.

[14] For ritual purification after menses. Some scholars place the mikvah before the synagogue in terms of importance to the community; you can worship outside, but if you don't have a suitable mikvah pool, nobody is allowed lawful intercourse.

NAAMAN, HEALED[15]

He ran back to the prophet's tent a different person, breathless and thankful. He pressed a reward on Elisha: clothes, silver,[16] jewelry. The prophet refused. Naaman tried again; transactions were what he understood. But Elisha would not be moved.

Then Naaman asked Elisha something; we never discussed this in Sunday school. He requested "two mules' burden of earth" to take with him, so that he could worship Elisha's God back in Syria. "Thy servant," he pledged, "will henceforth offer neither burnt offering nor sacrifice unto other gods, but unto the Lord." And Elisha allowed it.

Why would he need that earth? Isn't worship valid no matter what ground underlies it?

But I think I understand what Naaman wanted: something to build a fire on, something to soak the blood and fat of sacrifice. Clay pulls human, as like attracts like; it's a recognition of kinship.[17] Yes, you can change your life in a place where you are a stranger. But to make that change permanent, you have to take it home. Things that happen in other places feel transient, even though they may not be. Naaman needed a measure of his adopted country to carry back with him.

There is nothing to indicate that he returned the Hebrew servant to her family.

UNDERWATER TOWN
(JOCASSEE RIVER VALLEY, SOUTH CAROLINA)

Early in the morning, fishing boats drift through the mist that rises from the lake. Sometimes an eighteen-wheeler barrels

---

[15] 2 Kings 5:17.
[16] One talent equals seventy-five pounds.
[17] I explained to my lover that if we were to marry, it would have to be in South Carolina, at the foot of a sacred mountain. Otherwise, it wouldn't take.

across the far bridge, invisible in the fog, the *blat* of its brakes carrying over the water. And then it is quiet for a long time. Misleading to call the towns lost: we know right where they are, far below the lake's silver skin, below the boats' keels. At the bottom of Jocassee, of reservoirs like it, lie abandoned farmhouses that are always dark, attic to basement.

The diver stretches her arms above her head, making herself a blade, and launches herself with the balls of her feet. She pushes against the water with lean legs, not turning her masked face to look at the schools of sunnies and bass, pulling down with even strokes, breathing slowly through the tank. By now the water's brown-green, darker with each push, more substantial. Water compresses her to a smaller self. She snaps on her light, swimming slowly now, and when the farmhouse appears, pale clapboards rising out of the darkness, it surprises her again. She goes inside.

Nothing's changed, as far as she can tell. Silt cants against the baseboards, a straight-backed chair stands in a corner. Strips of wallpaper ripple in the gentle current. The windows are broken, probably by other divers, not the water that rose when the power company finished the dam and the river swelled, the footpaths flooded and the waterfalls straightened out, and the lake inched up barbed-wire fences and tree trunks, and further.

What if she stripped everything away? Her hair would lift and spread, a dark bloom in the water. Fecundity, life, sex. This, the powerful body that bears her, is what the world sees; hidden within there's a city whose streets she walks alone.[18] She doesn't need to be cleansed: preposterous idea. This mud, her own, washes her. She swims to the lake bottom because she can. Silver pillows of air issue from her lips, rise.

---

[18]Lights flash, small and bright, on the surface.

III.

Crescent City Beach

Over time the dead seal turns to beach, and nobody notices. Girls jog over the bones: mosaic of glass, gray stone, windfall knocked clean of twig, root, splinter. Flesh falls away and the ribs gleam, stripped of meat, pale ivory polished by grit. The skull, storm cellar, fills with stone tubers, each fitted close to its neighbor, spaces packed with straw and leaf, tamped carefully by tide. The empty eye socket swells with water, its divot a pool floored with bone, rimmed with thin smears of algae. And here, next to the skull, flipper bones arch—whole, articulate— angling from the wrist, tipped by four milky claws.

I want those claws, oval moons thralled, tied to the flipper's near coast—rubbed stone, bone lozenge, tablet, tooth. If I hold them under my tongue, will they melt there? Will they help me recall what it is to cut a spiral through hard waves, tear wriggling life apart and drain it down my throat, split water wide, haw a bark into the loud wind? Oh, I want them, silent claws, knocked, made beautiful by hard use. The jetty's living seals tumble, pillow- jostle, buck, bellow, stare at me, onyx eyed. What do they want? True, I have much worth coveting: incisors' blunt spades, breath's twinned wrung sponge, heel bone a hammer, hair a net sieve, jaw's fierce club, cochlea steeped in raw light. Overhead, gulls: tin cut from lighter tin. Lowering sky a hammered sheet.

Dead seal, you need nothing of mine; you have nothing to warrant my keeping. Your stones are not mine to touch, though they pull me, bed of my bone, bone of my nail—pull, yes, like the old fields, south and north, where my dear ones lie, taking their rest, laid over with swansdown snow or soaked by warm rains, safe from tide and storm, wrapped tight, dull glowings in that darkness.

Fossil

A fern's dark print on shale. Ribbed clamshells pressed into a cliff of pale limestone. The compliant trilobite in all its variations, every bump and ridge preserved these two hundred million years, yet still capable of revelation, like a pair of sneakers dangling from the power line, pedaling the silent air.

In the fossil room at the natural history museum, I especially like visiting the coprolite display, the ancient specimens of dung carefully laid out and labeled. That of the carnivorous reptiles looks intentional, shapely, like hunched figurines of forgotten idols. The grass-eater *Mesohippus,* ancestor of the horse, left flat patties stippled with bits of hay—a humble legacy, but one which has lasted longer than anything our kind has managed to create.

Near the coprolite, in a slab of what looks like pale sandstone, a fossil from what we now call Arizona: spider tracks, *Octopodichnus didactylus,* 240 million years old. It takes imagination to read the track: scattered pips and drags, then a faint scuff, as of a dragged body. A sweep of a finger would have obliterated it, or a breath of wind. And yet this little scrawl, characters spelling *death* and *dinner,* has survived. The same case holds a glowing knob of polished amber, lit from beneath by an electric bulb; inside swims a cockroach, trapped for thirty million years, oval wings and thin antennae familiar as this morning's garbage: *Blattidae.*

Walking through the museum, I think of the living fossils, lone survivors of once-populous families. Among trees, the star-leaved sweet gum, *Liquidambar,* valuable for salves and lump perfumes; the ginkgo, whose fluted leaves, in autumn, turn golden as chanterelles; the cycad, relic of ancient rain forests, with its long, rattling leaves.

And I think of the coelacanth's dramatic story, that ancient fish which swam through the thick waters of the dinosaur age, 350 million years ago. Before the continents floated to their current spots, before the Rockies buckled and lifted over the plains; before glaciers dug the Great Lakes. Before, before, the coelacanth lived before. And had been extinct for seventy million years, or so scientists thought. Then, in December 1938, a fishing trawler caught a coelacanth off the coast of South Africa. Since then, many other specimens have been found, very much like their fossil ancestors. They use their lobed fins to swim backward and upside down, and to crawl across the ocean floor.

The coelacanth lives in deep water, near the bottom where fresh lava oozes between shifting tectonic plates and the sea bubbles and boils. If a coelacanth is brought to the surface, it explodes from decompression. Since the rediscovery of the coelacanth, the story spread that fluid taken from its notochord would bring longevity to those who drank it. So their population, never large, has seen a dramatic decline since 1989.

The coelacanth's revival presents a problem. Like the ivory-billed woodpecker—another creature we thought we'd lost—something remains, a tatter of hope. Now that we've found that which was lost, what will we do with it? Protect, abandon, research it? Donate it? Ignore it?

The call rings out: *Lazarus, come forth.* (*He has been dead three days*, says his practical sister; *by this time, he stinketh.*) An unsteady figure emerges from the dark tomb. *Unwrap the grave clothes and give him something to eat.* Cerements lying in a heap on the dusty ground, a clue for the vigilant to find, a scrap that tells the story.

The coelacanth swims in black water where the sea floor boils; he has survived. Fear the coelacanth for the hope he brings, alive when we had long thought him dead. Which is more cruel, to let the family grieve, or to bring the lost one back, knowing he will die a second time? What if we kill the ancient thing again, this time forever? Certain now that this will be the death that takes.

Pepper's Junk Store

Old lawn mowers crowded the porch, and rusty bikes leaned against the columns. Inside, it was dim and dingy; an overhead fluorescent sputtered in the very back, where the tools were stacked, but if there were any other lights in the place, I don't remember them ever being turned on. Once our eyes adjusted, we could make out the narrow path that led from the door to the place where Mr. Pepper sat in state behind the jewelry counter, watching Clemson football on a grainy black-and-white television. If he'd heard us come in, he greeted us. If not, we made enough noise for him to know we were there, over the sports announcer's lonesome rattle. Mr. Pepper was a thin man with a high forehead, tallish and fragile, well into his eighties. His voice always surprised me: depth, splinters. He didn't seem to mind if we stayed all afternoon, and many times we did; often we had the place to ourselves.

At Pepper's store, browsing was spelunking. I had read about Aladdin's cave of wonders, and to me, seven years old, that place was it. The place was full of palpable magic from all the totems collected there. *National Geographics* in slippery spires. An old highboy whose contents I coveted for years: heavy turquoise jewelry, chokers and bracelets, nugget rings. Once, for my mother's birthday, I bought a pointed silver spoon, iridescent with tarnish, from Lebanon. Once, I bought a geode half, hollow as an Easter egg, its inside lined with dusty crystals I cleaned with an old toothbrush. Shark teeth and arrowheads, a quarter apiece, in Kerr jars. Tin brooch shaped like a pink chrysanthemum; human skull (was it real?); woolen uniform from Nazi Germany; manual typewriters with round, satisfying letter keys; a dull trombone, its slide frozen in place, nested in velvet.

Every time we went, I steeled myself to go farther. I was small and could wind through the narrow aisles between magazine cairns, bookshelves, and office tables bowed with boxes and crates. A sheaf of yardsticks; a silk flower floating inside a perfume bottle, a silvery bubble of air at the top. Dad spent hours going through bins of nails and bolts, bundles of twine, copper wire, narrow-gauge chain. He used a bundle of Pepper's cord to make a clothesline for my mother, and stashed bolts away in coffee cans, to wait decades for a use.

What I couldn't see I imagined: pale fish living in the store's dark corners, eyespots shrunk to pinpricks from generations of disuse; white spiders with elongated, whiplike legs sensitive to movement, not light. Certainly there were silverfish, swelled with gorging on softening newspapers and encyclopedia; certainly rodents of many kinds, nesting behind piles of pitchforks and axe handles, lining their beds with shreds of insulation from coils of ancient electrical cord.

We knew that Mr. Pepper liked us, and that made a difference. We had seen him refuse to sell to someone he disliked or didn't know, or charge a ridiculously high price. One man bought a barber chair, a big, heavy thing with aqua vinyl pads and a chrome footrest. He paid a lot for it. Mr. Pepper despised him; we could tell by the way he watched the man wrestle the chair out the door. But he showed us, once, his secret stash of Native artifacts, which he kept in a locked safe behind his counter. A tomahawk with a leather grip, painted pottery bowls, strings of trade beads. He asked us not to tell anyone about these things; he showed them only to dealers, he said. We could respect that. It was his safety in question. He was, by that time, an old man.

After leaving Pepper's, everything in the outside world looked different: less crowded, better lit, cleaner. *Wash your hands,* my mother ordered, *and leave those shoes at the door. You smell like that place.* But I liked to lift things carefully and peer at them, to wonder where they came from and what their story was. After leaving, my eyes ached with the strain of taking it all in.

Years later, after Mr. Pepper died, his relatives—he had no children—held an auction to empty the store. It took the auctioneers six months to arrange things in lots, and the auction lasted four weekends, one of the defining events of that summer. I was home from college and went myself. The old trade beads I had seen years earlier sold for better than four hundred dollars, as did an original broadside advertisement for Buffalo Bill's Wild West Show. I bid on, and won, an American flag with moth holes and forty-eight stars, as well as a brown concertina that now sits on my mantel, better than a thousand miles away from that old store next to the railroad. My parents bought the auction's biggest white elephant: two rooms stacked to the rafters with furniture and metal parts. They had a week to salvage what they could—a carved settee with horsehair stuffing coming out of the cushions, rusty Leaf-Lard cans, a rare straight-eight aluminum head for a certain kind of Buick. They had to pitch most of the stuff, but I still have a few things. A custard cup hangs in my kitchen; an awl, shorter than my little finger, with a brass knob like a pea and a sharp steel point, lies on my desk.

Pepper's store was the first museum I knew. The hoarder-king ruled over it all, and passed some of his habits to me; I breathed them in with the rich and dusty air. I find myself stooping on sidewalks, picking up nails and pocketing them. An old Noxzema jar fills with them, one by one. And at the Minneapolis Institute of Art, in the Africa room, a wooden figure bristles with pins and barbs, each nail representing a conflict spoken and resolved, an episode in the life of the town. What in it thrills me with recognition? These symbols of shared history, in what would look, to others, like refuse.

In the Country of Rent and Tatter

PROLOGUE: LAP QUILT

Black the ribbed shell of the rhino beetle laboring up the hill, black his armored legs, and black his overlarge bulldog's head, all shiny, hard black like lacquered metal, and fine ginger hairs lining his collar like an imperial ruff. Silver beads strung on a new spiderweb; in its middle, the lemon-tipped spider. Iridescent blue for the damselfly's steel body, needle slender and flicking. Tomato red for the sticky-skinned eft, on land for the only time in his life, standing out against the damp leaves like a live coal; soon he'll turn brown as bark, but now he blazes like Pentecostal tongues.

THE STITCHED MAP

Take this scrap of cloth, cotton, nothing fancy: Pickens County, South Carolina. Stretch it taut and tack a little stitch, tack, tack, tack. Call this corner the town at the foot of the mountain; call these hash marks the railroad, furrow from which the town sprouted. Because the railroad, then the market. Because the market, the textile mills. Because the mills, the jobs. Cotton cloth, bolt after bolt. Most of the mills stand idle now, but one I know spins woolen yarn for pricey sport socks; at Christmas, the workers get one free pair. The waste—yarn ends, lint, tracked-in dirt—they pack into bales and sell to a man who makes car carpet. Nothing is lost.

Say the running seams are curving highways, and follow this one south (I trace the thread with my finger) through downtown, where Robinson's still sells shoes and belts and dresses, where the old theater, now a church, pulls in a few folks for Sunday service. Here's the bank, my red-brick high school, the new post office. But here, in the strip mall, the thread snarls; avoid that route if you can. Follow this seam north, the mountain road, follow it out of town and through the foothills.

Spread out this scrap of cotton, smooth it on your knees. Run your fingers over the stitched highways, the railroad line, the knotted town. This edge the mountains, and this one the state line. Oh, there's work in this, flashing needle, floss tied and bitten, and before that, someone tending a flexing heddle, shooting the shuttle forward and back as warp and woof stacked. Imagined this way, it seems easy—seconds tick, the plain cloth grows—though it wasn't. But unmaking it would be a dream; pull threads and watch the edge recede, pick at a frayed knot and lift it clean away.

The Town at the Foot of the Mountain

Hummock of clay stuck full of church steeples, like pins in a cushion. Inside, the people turn onionskin pages when the preacher names the text, and the church fills with the sound of rustling rain. From childhood I was among that number, sitting straight on the red-cushioned pew. At night I could lull myself to sleep by reciting the names of the sixty-six books. *He has made everything beautiful in its time; also he has set the world in their heart.* Yes. Here's where I'm from, where I wasn't born but born again, redeemed before I had a chance to do much to repent of. Ever since I have loved these mountains with the zeal of a convert.

Summer on the Mountain

I took a job on the mountain overlooking the town. I lived in the barracks by the campground, and in the mornings I took people out in canoes on the lake, afternoons led craft programs

and used the captive corn snake to teach campers about reptiles, evenings imitated the screech owl's cry in hopes he would
hoot back, while I talked in a hushed voice about the adapta-
tions of night hunters. When I wasn't giving programs, I read
field guides in the nature center, learned about mushrooms
and mixed oak-hickory forests, chestnut blight, beetles, how to
skin and stuff a mouse. Days off, I searched in vain for the rare
Oconee bell, and late at night, I drove the park road and saw
the dark mountain silhouetted against the sky. *Home.* I felt it;
my home takes that mountain's shape.

QUILTER

She sat beside the highway all summer, selling jars of sourwood
honey and quilts draped over a clothesline. They swelled and
waved in the hot-wind gusts the big trucks made. I would show
you those scraps, swatches and tag ends stitched, backed with
ticking and stuffed with cotton batt. A ragbag stuffed with this
and that. When I dream of the place it's always in color; I wrap
myself with it on cold nights.

SILVER

Start with the color of the highway carrying me there. Snip a tin
sheet for the lake's flashing skin, and for the water tower in town,
visible on a clear day. Pearl for the snail's track and pewter for
his body, sensitive lead-colored horns drawing in whenever he
bumps something. Aluminum fishhooks dangling from snarled
line, snatches of shed snakeskin caught in a tree crotch, iron-
tasting water pouring from the faucet into my cup, my tin cup.

ORANGE

For the jewelweed's bloom, red throat and sun-spattered petals;
orange for the turk's cap lily, streaked with paprika, and yellow
for the pollen it drops. Orange for clumps of little mushrooms,

their caps dimpled like red blood cells; the orange-tipped assassin beetle's crest and beak, syringe-like, with which he pierces prey. Orange lichen splashed across granite, patiently crumbling stone to sand, orange needles on the beetle-killed pines, orange peaches ripening on the twisted trees in the valley, orange-headed lightning beetles, orange clay bearing it all up. Orange bands on the corn snake we kept in the nature center, striped with rust and dead leaf and twig; obsidian black his lidless eye.

PINK

For the water lily's throat, which a hapless mother noticed on an early canoe float: "I don't WANT to look at the stupid water lilies!" the teen screamed, rocking the canoe with dangerous force.

CRIMSON

Berries of creeping squaw-weed, cap of fly agaric, campfire embers glowing on silent parents, their children asleep in a nylon tent. Red for the beanie the pileated woodpecker wears as he hammers the dead pine snag, strips of bark tumbling down. Hearts-a-bustin', its bright orange seeds surrounded by a studded fuchsia pod. Red and white bobbers hanging like cherries in the low-growing alders on the lakeshore. Dark theater-curtain red for the roadside sumac, whose velvet seed cluster I steeped in cold water to make pink lemonade. Red-hearted watermelon, bloody gash in the forehead of the hurt hiker. Pokeweed red-purple as rhubarb, tall as trees, white cotton inside its stalk, sharp smell when broken, and purple juice from its berries, growing on the side of the road.

JAGGED SEAM

The eastern continental divide is here, stitching the country together, a running seam on the bias. If a drop of rain falls here, it will end up in the Gulf of Mexico; if it falls here, just east, it will wind through mountains and foothills, percolate through midlands and into marshes where salt- and sweet-water mingle, trickle into the ocean, laving the little coquina clams, bright pink or yellow or purple, that dig in the beach's hard-packed sand.

Black

And white for the turkey vulture who lives there, as he lives in the rest of the lower forty-eight, a common, practical bird. I used to lie on the cold granite mountaintop, watching him glide with his wide wings, and think of his bare neck, better for plunging into road-killed deer; his sense of smell, rare among birds; his wattles, painted with gore. Judicious, the vulture wastes nothing, hanging on thermal currents to conserve energy, scanning the ground; he makes his living on what we pretend's beneath our notice.

Once, after rain, I watched a dozen tiger swallowtails (velvety black, studded with teal, plum, pollen sequins) poke a pile of waterlogged dog shit with their soda-straw tongues, sucking out nutrients. Yes, butterflies like flowers, but not as well as sweat, or urine, or rotting fruit deliquescing into a puddle on the ground. These swallowtails stood on no ceremony; they ate what they could and flew off when a little boy ran over to see what the fuss was about. The butterflies were black as the racer snake who shot into a clump of grass at my approach; black like my barracks room at night, no streetlight's glow to mark the window's lighter square. Biotite mica flecking the creek bed, dark hemlock trunks on damp mornings, black cracks netting dogwood bark. Black ants racing across bare granite, hell-bent on going somewhere. Black-masked Canada geese, raising their young by the lake; week after week I watched the juveniles grow, until I could not tell them from their parents. Crows squawking in the trees, social and smart, unpopular; berries shiny as jet.

YELLOW

Striping the bodies of the hornets, who darted into the port-hole of the nest they built in the fork of a hemlock tree. The yellowroot's cadmium stems, shining out like candle flame when I scratched their thin bark, bound in bundles and sold for medicinal tea. Yellow for the raw acorns squirrels dropped, brass-yellow rings on Mason jars full of sourwood honey, and moonlight pale yellow for the honey inside. Yellow patterns on the carapace of the box turtle, which scientists think may be more territorial than we knew: when the turtles are released any distance from the place of their birth, they roam endlessly in search of home.

BLUE

Ripe huckleberries, hidden under a canopy of oval leaves along the ridgeline, where the air hums with bees and smells of pine needles baking in the sun all day. Here, near the summit, I heard a denim-shirted man read the Sermon on the Mount to a group of teenagers. They were hiked-out and sweaty, dirt-smudged but attentive, and they gazed behind him at the green mountains rippling below. Blue for the *Indigo lactarius,* a mushroom that bleeds sapphire drops when cut, gills of pleated lapis. Blue for the wings of the kingfisher speeding low over the lake, crying *cuk cuk cuk*; blue for the great heron that needs a long runway to take flight (six-foot wingspan), finally rising, flapping hard, glints in its yellow eye. Faded chalky blue of the diving plat-form, anchored in the deep water; I watched a boy cannonball off the high dive as his friends screamed *suicide, suicide.* Blue for the lake itself, reflecting the summer sky; blue-flagged patio by the lodge, where I sat with my kayakers while mist rose from the lake. Flagstones of blue granite, which the Civilian Conservation Corps cut and joined and laid.

In the 1930s, the CCC boys worried granite from clay, carried stones heavy as meal sacks up the mountain, chipped hollows mimicking the contours of each stone's underneath, and rocked each stone into place, tamping it down with their weight. Hard work for a dollar a day, and they were glad to get it. They sent it down the mountain to their families in Easley, Pickens, Sunset Community, Nine Times.

Praise be to the Corps, who split logs and shake-shingled the cabins, dug the lake and dammed Carrick Creek, poured footers, tied strings to stake the place where the lodge would stand. They raised the bathhouse and the chapel in the woods. They chipped toeholds in Governor's Rock, making it possible to summit without technical gear. They painted blue blazes on tree trunks to mark the way. And when their season's work was done, they dismantled their bunkhouse at the mountain's foot, stacking the scarred boards for some future use.

White

Mist rising from the field by the river as we stood, steaming, catching our breath from dancing on the springy barn floor, in that place that smelled of sweat and hops, sandalwood, mice. White blossoms of the mountain laurel and maypop; white for the dress of the bride I saw ducking into the shake-shingle chapel in the woods, a warm, rainy night early in July, water dripping from the pine boughs as she drew the door shut behind her. Years later I would walk through the same door, a bride myself. White stems and blossom of Indian pipe, a plant with no chlorophyll. The pale stem and cap of destroying angels and death caps, mushrooms pushing up through leaf litter. Club fungi, the color of old piano keys, growing from a rotting log: dead man's fingers. White hominy we ate together around the barracks table; two white refrigerators, one for food, the other for beer and bait.

On a cool August evening, barracks windows open for the breeze, music drifted into the living room: "America the Beautiful." A high-school band was staying at the Methodist camp down the road. I was sitting on the sofa with J., my barracks mate, whom I cared for. Absently, he rubbed the sole of my foot while he read. I stitched a pattern of indigo flowers on a white pillowcase. The band started and stopped, practicing a few bars until they got it right. The soft sigh of thread as I pushed it through the cotton, pulled it out the other side. When the old refrigerator cycled on, the lamp flickered; millers beat themselves against the window screens, desperate to get at the light inside. I felt, simply, content. Then the music stopped, and I tied off my thread, slipping the needle into the cloth to save.

Love Song

I see you in the pair of jet earrings I buy, the same hard black as the beetle; I deck myself with you. The pomegranate seed's the same ruby as the bolete that pushes from the leaf litter. The co-op sells clay for $15.80 a pound, four times more expensive than steak—sifted white and green clays from France, next to an article about geophagy, and chili powder the color of the cloddy earth I know. Clay in a damp poultice eases sting or fever, makes bones strong, scrubs muddy blood, eases aching bellies. Even when the child within is the size of a pea, the women know to eat clay. They cannot hush their bodies' insistent whisper.

Orange

But with every hike to the summit I see another clear-cut—another slash of red clay with edges square as a grave—in the acres east and south of here.

Green

Most of all, green the background on which everything else is stitched. Kudzu lining the neglected roadsides, twining over standing pines. After the first frost, the vines die back, dead streamers hanging. But with spring the kudzu returns, its three-part leaves turning pine snags to columns, making a temple with no roof, like—not too much of a stretch—the Greek ruins at Paestum, south of Rome, fluted columns rising into the air, striped lizards sunning themselves on the old hewn steps. I spent a long afternoon there, shivering in the March wind, amazed at having the ruins to myself, twenty, wondering what it all meant. And yet the kudzu is more mysterious and threatening. It carpets the field with leaves, but what creeps beneath? In the deep summer shade, the very air green, the leaves are like water of uncertain depth. It's easy to imagine stepping in and having the green slowly close over your head. Vines anchor themselves to limb stubs, send out suckers and hold fast. Runners tack and climb, drape and preserve, glorify.

▨ ▨ ▨

Maybe scraps are all we've ever had; threads of mycelium working through forest duff, a woman made from a crumb of clay. *These fragments I have shored*, these pieces I have squirreled away. I have wished for sharper ears to hear the rasp of wasp chewing wood into paper, to hear water pumping through the arteries of thin-barked beech trees. Have wished for a body more sensitive, to feel the slow swelling of yeasty lava that lifts the mountain a little more every day. Sometimes I swear I can feel the earth rising, bearing me up.

Archaeology of Lost Women

> This is a mammal paleontologist's nightmare, the
> dreaded "harmonica," or a jaw without teeth. Without
> teeth, it's often impossible to determine precisely what
> the creature is.
>
>
>
> INTERPRETIVE DISPLAY, MINNESOTA
> SCIENCE MUSEUM, ST. PAUL
>
>

We know little about her, save her name. We know little about
her, but she worked in a textile mill. We know little about her,
but she washed sheets in a hospital, cared for her husband after
his stroke, lived out her life in this place.

Even the women whose blood I share are unknown to me
as the names in a county ledger. What am I supposed to do,
not wonder about their lives, stick to my own story? No. I will
scour histories and sift facts, read about soil content and av-
erage annual income. I follow their recipes (three years and
I could afford meat only twice); I unfold their dress patterns
(which material will last longest and show the least wear?). Too
few of them could spare time to write journals or letters, and
too many of those notes lie crumbling in a back room, shredded
into mouse nests. Here I am showing you my sleights. Little
bones. I tell it as I believe it could have been, how my own life
has shown me. I'll presume to speak for them. Fault me, try to
shut your ears, and still I'll say, as said the God of Zipporah and
Hagar and Leah: Give me a rib and I'll give you a woman.

Three Relics

PORCELAIN BABY. *OHIO, AD 1975*

Although I've had the porcelain baby as long as I can remember, its details still surprise me: navel pocking the belly's swell, throat's tiny divot, spine furrowing the narrow back. Small as a knuckle, white as sun-bleached bone, the porcelain baby stares calmly from two brush-tick pupils, carmine lips pursed firmly. Daubs of dark lead mark the place where limbs once attached. A raised seam runs the body's length, remnant of the mold, and just under the left ear I can see where someone scraped away a bit of still-malleable porcelain; this proof of human touch may be the detail I like best.

Many years ago, as my mother tilled her garden, preparing the plot for sowing, the machine's blade churned something small and white from the soil. She dropped it in her pocket and washed it under a faucet in the old farmhouse where they lived then, built in 1865 on slabs of hewn granite and held together with thick pegs.

One afternoon, the phone in the kitchen rang; the doctor confirmed what she'd suspected: pregnancy. She cried, she admits now, overwhelmed, though they knew they wanted children. Her husband, my father, was up on the roof, nailing a loose shingle. He climbed slowly down the ladder and they began to make their plans. It was mid-May, and the lilac bush by the back door was in bloom.

Not many weeks later, something passed from her, shapeless, clotted. Was she relieved? But the doctor's ultrasound showed that the baby was unharmed. Twins ran in her family; could she have borne two? She, I, will never know. What of the lost twin, the double self, unmourned and unburied, lost? The bone baby won't say. Some cannot be saved.

There's something idolatrous about the porcelain baby; something in the muscled little body demands tribute. It could be Jesus, of course. It's the right size for a crèche, and something in the eyes calculates, prepares for disappointment. The limbless Christ, dark metal where legs and arms should join; so long without limbs, it seems complete without them. Its pointed pelvis forms something like a stake or a spear.

The earth there yields teeth, arrowheads, pottery shards, and, once, this bit of molded bone, turned and shaped and painted: an inscrutable torso, small and easily missed, bobbing like pumice in the raw soil. When blade cuts turf, long-planted offspring rise. All these clues read, *Someone lived here before you,* and also, *Dust, dust.* But this bone-china baby, what does it say? *New life is pointed like a spade, and brief;* and, *Yours is not the only life.* Discarded, priceless fragment, saying, *Be mindful where you step. Carry your shoes in your hand.*

RECIPE. *MINNESOTA, AD 2003*

One winter afternoon, a month after our wedding, I was paging through one of his cookbooks when a folded piece of paper slipped out. I picked it up off the floor, opened it, and immediately it was as though she stood in my kitchen, our kitchen, his lover before me, in that handwritten recipe. We had been speaking acquaintances once, but when word got around, she would pass me as though I were not there. This pained me, but I would not approach her. When he left she had paid for the right to hold me in contempt. I knew too that I would have done the same.

I held it in my hand, this recipe that her mother must have written—the list of ingredients and the body of directions in a hand I did not recognize, marginal notes in a hand I did. We had moved better than a thousand miles north, far from the kitchen they had once shared, where she had stood over a counter and parsed out spices, where she had seared poultry in a hot skillet. And in that long move we had brought with us this single sheet of paper, this relic from a time they shared.

I threw it away without a thought. That was past. I would not have her words in my place, in the apartment he and I struggled with every paycheck to rent. Finding this thing she had made was like finding a picture of them together, the two of them sitting on a white-painted porch swing, his arm circling her shoulders, her head inclined toward him, their faces lit with happiness. He had loved another, and it had not lasted: here was physical evidence, as if I needed it. Understand, I wished her no ill, but I wanted no ghost in my house.

And yet after I had thrown the recipe away, I regretted it. I knew he loved that dish—chicken with molé sauce—and believed I could make it better than she had. Why hadn't I kept it? I looked up the recipe in a cookbook, made a list of ingredients, and went to the supermarket. Cocoa powder, dried plums, chiles, plum tomatoes. I minced shallots fine and sautéed them in butter, and on another burner dark sauce bubbled.

But this was a futile exercise. We are not different, we two who have shared one man. How many of her turns of phrase linger in his speech, how many gestures? How many times in a day does some trigger turn his mind back? I cannot begrudge him this, for this is riches, to have lived, as now, before, to have been to another what he is to me.

But hear this, all you who cannot know what I have staked on my love for this man. I will not leave, he who has been to me a cruse of water and a cake of meal in a starving time, he whose body I have fed so often and so well that even if he left me, listen, even if then, part of me would remain; flesh remembers, even if mind forgets, what once made it strong. *Love is stronger than death, passion more fierce than the grave.* Hear me. If we had nothing left but bone and water, I could feed him on that, make marrow-dark broth rich enough to steady him for this day's work.

FALSE DOOR. *EGYPT, GIZA, 2400 BCE*

When the priest fell ill for what the physicians knew would be the last time, one of them sent a temple boy to the stone-cutter, who counted off dimensions, held his chisel above the stone, and struck. The limestone split evenly; it was a propitious day for this kind of work. The stonecutter positioned his chisel again.

Early the next day, the scribe arrived, unrolling his set of delicate picks and chisels from a linen wrapper. The dying man wanted what they all wanted: his name repeated many times, to ensure the survival of his *ka*; pleas to passersby, imploring food offerings, or asking them to say the prayers that would cause food to materialize in the world of the dead.

The priest lay on his deathbed, listening, shivering although the sun—the last he would see—was high overhead. The sharp chipping of limestone, he knew, was the scribe carving the proper glyphs on the false door of his tomb-chapel. Through this portal his *ka* would pass to partake of offerings left to him.

It would be a duty of the temple boys to fish for him in the river, dropping their nets into the shallow water and jerking them up quick to snare the little silver-skinned fishes. These they pierced with bone knives, sand-sharpened, and let the entrails spill on the ground. One of the temple dogs would lick them up. The boys spread the flayed bodies of the fish on the drying rack, and while one—steady-handed—lifted carefully the spines from flesh, another waved sticks to keep ravens and vultures away. The desert afternoon dried the fish quickly, and the setting sun found the boys packing earthen jars with alternating layers of white, coarse-grained salt and pale fish flesh. They heated a stick of wax over a flame and ran it over the jar's mouth, pressed the lid down. Beads of wax bubbled around the seal. The boys blew out the flame and made ready to go to the old priest's tomb. Once he had his meal, they could have theirs. Thinking of these things, knowing that he would be provided for, the old priest died at peace, and was entombed.

Time passed. All of them, farmers and traders alike, brought their tax to the temple. Dates, almonds, olive oil, barley, wine. The boys placed flasks and plates by the door of the old priest's tomb. His diet was varied even if some days the plates seemed untouched. Was it not his prerogative to go hungry, if he chose so, in the afterlife? Sometimes they lingered, daring each other to trace the images of his name—bird, eye, snake—and sometimes they were silent, thinking of different things. One cursed the bird who had pecked him earlier, by the fish racks, so that his hand bled and he had to wrap a cloth around it. One thought of his mother, whom he barely remembered, but associated in his mind with the kohl dealers who sometimes gathered outside the temple door. She had lined her eyes with kohl, dipping the delicate pencil into the squat cosmetic pot, focusing on her face reflected in a circle of polished bronze. One thought of the water snake he had seen swimming across the current in the river, pointed toward the far shore. He could not look away.

He would expect this, the old priest—had he not done the same himself as a boy?—the priest, long dead, the careful offerings brought by successive generations of temple boys, some thoughtful and some perfunctory, as the upper world swung through year after year until his name was forgotten, year after year until sand obscured his tomb and wore down his temple, year after year until someone hooked chains and pulleys to his chapel door and hove. The limestone broke loose of its ancient footings. Someone wrapped the door in canvas and set it in a frame; someone loaded the huge crate onto a ship. This he could not have foreseen.

Now the door is displayed, in a room filled with other artifacts, at the Minneapolis Institute of Art. I make it my errand
to visit. Iry-en Akhet, Lector-Priest, what would he think if
one bright afternoon he passed through this portal, expecting
to find dried fish or barley bread, and found me instead, taking
notes with a plastic pen, faintly backlit by the case on the op-
posite wall, a case full of tortoiseshell hair combs, faience pen-
dants, glass cosmetic bottles in which the last remains of lotion
and paint still cling? If this can last, why not his temple, why
not his god?

INCANTATION

You, stranger, lend me the breath in your throat; say the word
and I will be fed. It costs you a passing moment, no more, only
time, next to nothing. It does not rob your mouth of meat, does
not empty your stomach of cud. Say the word. You, living, cannot know hunger like mine. Like you, I remember feast days:
leeks and crackling fat, wine, honey dripping on barley bread.
Now, dead, hunger swallows me whole; I burn with it as a candle flame. You, stranger! Speeched, you have power, can speak
into existence food such as living tongues have never tasted,
stoneless fruit, yielding flesh, satiety without excess, please; say
the word. I was once like you. You cannot yet know the sharp
hunger of the dead.

The Body as Reliquary

In our bodies as we walk or lie, we're stretched over bones laved with blood and water, precious and practical branches of leg or bits of finger. How fascinated I used to be by the reliquaries in Italian cathedrals, elaborately worked gold set with sapphires and embossed into intricate designs, the crystal pane protecting a splinter of wood or tatter of cloth.

In the wet collection, too, a part comes to stand for the whole. A dead crawfish in alcohol, looking as though carved from horn or bone, conjures the knobby stones over which the live creature crawled, the icy water it breathed; the low-hanging rhododendron whose shade dappled the water, the rat snake expertly climbing the tree, black-and-white belly scales gripping the bark. The sky above darkened, and a mountain storm broke. Wind stripped a branch from a hemlock and flung it into the creek. The crawfish waved its antennae and backed under the shadow of a stone as the water danced.

The fish from the Rogue River. I saw it in the wet collection. A big fish, maybe eighteen inches long, bent to fit in a tall jar with a glass lid. Collected 1898. I don't remember the species, but I remember the curator speculating that the fish is probably extinct now, because it lived in a microclimate. Probably a single bight in the river. The river, as it was, is gone; so is the collector, bent over the blazing water. This is precious because it's all we have.

I Keep a Jar of Clay Beside My Bed

The bones of the women waked them, nights, crying for iron. While the houses slept, the women slipped out of their beds and unhooked their doors, eased them open and shut. They rubbed the warm skulls of the hounds, who quieted. Bare feet slapped the creek path. They knelt on the bank and scooped handfuls of clay, squatting, so as not to dirty their night dresses. Red clay slick between their teeth. They ate it from their hands. How they craved it, night and day, their bones aching for it. Mornings they dropped rusty nails in the stew, evenings they fried beans in a cast iron skillet shiny with rubbed fat, ever they gazed at their children through gray mists of anemia. All this though the earth bearing them was rich with the rust that made it a fight to grow anything there. Squash didn't fill, corn shriveled. Greens bolted, turned tough and bitter. But how that clay did grow women, women pale and thin, women waking early in hot sheets, with stained soles and knees and hands. Marked no matter how they scrubbed. How it tugged them from bed late at night, alone, and they never spoke of it. How it fought with their bones. I know, for it pulls me now.

■ ■ ■

In the book of Judges, I read about the massacre of the Ephraimites, who picked a fight with the Gileadites and then tried to escape. But the Gileadites caught them at the river and said, *Ye are fugitives,* and said, *Say now Shibboleth,* which meant ear of corn, or stream in flood, from *shabal,* to flow. They said, again, *Say now Shibboleth,* and the Ephraimites said *Sibboleth:* "for they could not frame it to pronounce it right." Forty-two thousand slain that day, betrayed by accent, and Jordan's stream swelled with dark blood. Not for the first time; not for the last.

※ ※ ※

My password is any word containing "oi," vowels tucked between supple consonants, the word heavy with fuel for the growing, corn in full ear, kernels packed in silk. *Coil* sounds like *coal, foil* like *foal.* When I am home, these words smooth my path. But I have been away so long.

Stretch out your hand, the left one, the one belonging to the devil. A triangle spreads in your palm. My home, the seam angling between thumb and forefinger, is printed on every hand. The thumb's ball makes Georgia, the flat below fingers North Carolina, the hand's edge the seacoast. South Carolina in the middle, blood-warm and damp, rooted by tendons. Say the names of the wrinkled rivers: Santee, Saluda, Cooper, Congaree. Open your hand, and if you will not, keep it closed, put it fisted behind you, and listen. Let my slow speech give me away. My *soil* sounds like *soul;* my home will ever fill my mouth. At night I say, *How could I ever forsake you.*

Epilogue

Becoming a Prophet

DEFINITION

It's not predicting the future, but saying what we know but won't accept. We're made of clay, and we smell of it, dampness funneling from our palms. Practice breaking news bluntly—apologies dull the blade. Learn to sit quietly; any place will do. Bus stop, library. I see my fellow prophets-in-training on the streets and recognize them by the way their eyes hold mine.

LOVE

His name a spell in my mouth. His body a sun-warmed rock the surf cast me upon. His mind a city I waited long to visit: patter in the marketplace, silence in sacred shadow. He is bright forsythia, ship's running light, seed of the world's oldest tree. His quiet sleep a desert in bloom.

READY

Gone the snap and hiss of the radiator, the map on the wall with its running stitch of sea routes, the stack of useful plates, eggs unbroken in their crate, the complacent jug of milk. Silenced the books on the shelf, and the books below them. I hang the walls with linen, plait a mat for the floor. I light a fire beneath the kettle. The dusty air dances, rich, in the gilded afternoon light.

COUNTRY

Walk through the woods, past mice gnawing antlers for the calcium, thickets of blackberry canes, crimson vines twisting up a pine snag. High in the dead tree, the lozenge-shaped hole the woodpecker pounded. At my feet, the pile of wood dust rasped by a termite colony. Dead branches creak in the wind; wind scours my face. Distractions abound. What do they teach?

City

The shop windows are living dioramas; behind the mannequins in whispering toiles, a shifting frieze of clerks and customers. The lunch crowd lingers over avocado salad, dishes smeared with leavings. Outside, a stoplight dangles like a pendant on a cord. Exhaust rafts from tailpipes. I must notice what others won't: on the sidewalk, yellow jackets swarm a bit apple.

What Work Awaits

There was once an old man, called "the Old Man," who had no feeling in his face, a quality that made him the ideal subject for many experiments. Duchenne du Boulogne (1806–1875), a scientist, clipped wires to the folds of the Old Man's cheeks, stimulated his facial muscles with electric shock, and photographed the results. Based on these experiments, he claimed that the Duchenne smile is the only one, of eighteen possible, to occur because of "simultaneously experienced enjoyment." The captions read, "Smile Caused by Electrical Shock," and "The Duchenne Smile." Is there any question which is the evil work? A false smile wrenched from the body by pain, even unfelt; I must strive against this.

Prayer

Late at night, the ceiling creaks with the steps of the restless lovers upstairs. Four blue pilots glow in the kitchen, the computer drive glimmers green, and outside, across the street, a floodlight sputters on blue snow. These are the votives of this place. I touch broom straw to burner and watch gray strands of smoke rise like the breaths of those who wait patiently in the cold. I would make all a supplication, lungs' each press and stretch.

DAILY OFFICE

Separate like from unlike, set and reset a timer. Move silently through the day, past the white blare of television, the consumptive sigh of passing cars. Bleach hums in the porcelain sink. Keen a blade with whetstone and oil, cut parallel furrows on the wooden block; make tile's graph gleam. I have tried to still my mind. This is work I have enjoyed, and do. Ropes of water unbraid from the spout.

Notes

The Wet Collection

My thanks to Rebecca Newberry at the Science Museum of Minnesota.

Jeremiad of a Bad Drought Year

Section 2. Ezekiel 37:1–14.

Section 6. II Samuel 23:13–17.

Building a Funeral

I have changed the names in this essay.

The Rain Follows the Plow

Barbara Allen, *Homesteading the High Desert* (Salt Lake City: University of Utah Press, 1987). The coffee-cup anecdote comes from one of the oral histories in this book.

"Appendix A—Provisional Vascular Plant List, The Island ACEC/RNA," (The Native Plant Society of Oregon, Oregon State University, and Prineville District BLM, June 8, 1996).

Phil F. Brogan, *East of the Cascades,* L.K. Phillips, ed. (Portland, OR: Binfords and Mort, 1964).

Jill A. Chappel, and Dawn Mankowski, "History of the Cove Palisades State Park," unpublished.

Alice Day Pratt, *A Homesteader's Portfolio,* Introd. Molly Gloss (Corvallis, OR: Oregon State UP, 1993. First published in 1922 by Macmillan).

Thanks also to Steve Janiszewski, manager of the Cove Palisades State Park during my time there, and to Paul Patton, interpretive ranger at Smith Rock State Park, both of the Oregon State Parks and Recreation Department, and well-versed in knowledge of the High Desert.

Little White House

See Doris Kearns Goodwin's excellent *No Ordinary Time: Franklin and Eleanor Roosevelt: The Home Front in World War II* for more about the Little White House. I took Eleanor's anecdote about Eisenhower from this book.

Second-String

I have changed the names in this essay.

Ave Maria Grotto

Jeremiah 23:29.

In the Country of Rent and Tatter

Ecclesiastes 3:11.

Thanks also to Scott Stegenga, interpretive ranger at Table Rock State Park in Pickens, South Carolina, a perceptive and thoughtful teacher.

Three Relics

Song of Songs 8:6.

I Keep a Jar of Clay Beside My Bed

Judges 12:1–7.

Acknowledgments

For grants and fellowships over the years, I would like to thank Inprint, the Creative Writing Program at the University of Houston, the Department of English and the Edelstein-Keller Endowment in Creative Writing at the University of Minnesota, and the Minnesota State Arts Board.

For reading earlier versions of these essays, I thank Mark Doty, Emily Fox Gordon, Kimiko Hahn, James Kastely, and Lynn Voskuil. Charles Baxter provided trenchant advice. Amanda Coplin, Laura Flynn, Braden Kerwin, and Rachel Moritz created generous community.

For their steadfast support, I thank my family, especially Earl and Margie Tevis, and Diantha Tevis. For sustenance emotional, spiritual, intellectual, and gastronomical, I thank Chad and Nancy Bissada Wilson; Michael and Mary Daniell Bryant; Julie Goolsby; and Valerie Jean Conner and Stan Makielski.

And thanks most especially to David Bernardy, strength and help, my dear one.

Some of these essays have appeared previously in the following magazines:

"Bigfoot's Widow," *Barrelhouse*

"Beyond the Wilderness," *North Dakota Quarterly*

"Ave Maria Grotto," *Southern Humanities Review*

"Barefoot in a Borrowed Corset" (as "Bather, Alone"), *Conjunctions*

"The Wet Collection," *Bellingham Review*

"Chihuahua Desert Love Song," *AGNI*

"I Keep a Jar of Clay Beside My Bed," *Shenandoah*

"Crescent City Beach," *Isotope*

"Second-String," *Dislocate*

"Building a Funeral," *The Southeast Review*

Formerly a park ranger, factory worker, and seller of cemetery plots, JONI TEVIS currently teaches literature and creative writing at Furman University in Greenville, South Carolina. Her essays have appeared in *Orion*, *The Oxford American*, *DIAGRAM*, and elsewhere. *The Wet Collection* is her first book.

Author photo by David Bernardy

ldman

ces

o#440 PPI paper

MORE BOOKS FROM MILKWEED EDITIONS

To order books or for more information, contact Milkweed at (800) 520-6455 or visit our Web site (www.milkweed.org).

Toward the Livable City
Edited by Emilie Buchwald

The Prairie in Her Eyes
Ann Daum

Boundary Waters:
The Grace of the Wild
Paul Gruchow

Grass Roots:
The Universe of Home
Paul Gruchow

Bird Songs of the Mesozoic:
A Day Hiker's Guide to the Nearby Wild
David Brendan Hopes

This Incomparable Land:
A Guide to American Nature Writing
Thomas J. Lyon

The Pine Island Paradox
Kathleen Dean Moore

The Barn at the End of the World:
The Apprenticeship of a Quaker, Buddhist Shepherd
Mary Rose O'Reilley

North to Katahdin:
What Hikers Seek on the Trail
Eric Pinder

Ecology of a Cracker Childhood
Janisse Ray

Wild Card Quilt:
The Ecology of Home
Janisse Ray

Back Under Sail:
Recovering the Spirit of Adventure
Migael Scherer

Of Landscape and Longing:
Finding a Home at the Water's Edge
Carolyn Servid

Homestead
Annick Smith

Interior design by Wendy H
Typeset in Adobe Caslon Pr
by Stanton Publication Serv
Printed on Recycled Cream
by Edwards Brothers, Inc.

MORE BOOKS FROM MILKWEED EDITIONS

To order books or for more information, contact Milkweed at
(800) 520-6455 or visit our Web site (www.milkweed.org).

Toward the Livable City
Edited by Emilie Buchwald

The Prairie in Her Eyes
Ann Daum

Boundary Waters:
The Grace of the Wild
Paul Gruchow

Grass Roots:
The Universe of Home
Paul Gruchow

Bird Songs of the Mesozoic:
A Day Hiker's Guide to the Nearby Wild
David Brendan Hopes

This Incomparable Land:
A Guide to American Nature Writing
Thomas J. Lyon

The Pine Island Paradox
Kathleen Dean Moore

The Barn at the End of the World:
The Apprenticeship of a Quaker, Buddhist Shepherd
Mary Rose O'Reilley

North to Katahdin:
What Hikers Seek on the Trail
Eric Pinder

Ecology of a Cracker Childhood
Janisse Ray

Wild Card Quilt:
The Ecology of Home
Janisse Ray

Back Under Sail:
Recovering the Spirit of Adventure
Migael Scherer

Of Landscape and Longing:
Finding a Home at the Water's Edge
Carolyn Servid

Homestead
Annick Smith

MILKWEED EDITIONS

Founded in 1979, Milkweed Editions is one of the largest independent, nonprofit literary publishers in the United States. Milkweed publishes with the intention of making a humane impact on society, in the belief that good writing can transform the human heart and spirit. Within this mission, Milkweed publishes in four areas: fiction, nonfiction, poetry, and children's literature for middle-grade readers.

JOIN US

Milkweed depends on the generosity of foundations and individuals like you, in addition to the sales of its books. In an increasingly consolidated and bottom-line-driven publishing world, your support allows us to select and publish books on the basis of their literary quality and the depth of their message. Please visit our Web site (www.milkweed.org) or contact us at (800) 520-6455 to learn more about our donor program.

Interior design by Wendy Holdman
Typeset in Adobe Caslon Pro
by Stanton Publication Services
Printed on Recycled Cream 50#440 PPI paper
by Edwards Brothers, Inc.